God Calls
Me Deb
and
Thank You
Elton John

By
Deborah Owens

God Calls Me Deb

&

Thank You, Elton John

Written by

Deborah Owens

"I asked God for all things

that I may enjoy life

He gave me life

that I may enjoy all things"

Table of Contents

INTRODUCTION

CHAPTER 1 - OH BOY! THIS IS SCARY

CHAPTER 2 – THE VISION

CHAPTER 3 - THE GIRL WITH HER HAIR IN A BUN

CHAPTER 4 - THE GIRL WITH HER FAMILY

CHAPTER 5 - CONSEQUENCE OF A MOMENT

CHAPTER 6 - INTRO TO ELTON JOHN

CHAPTER 7 - MY BRUTALITY

CHAPTER 8 - SEPARATING DEITY

CHAPTER 9 - THE GROOMING

CHAPTER 10 - HIGH SCHOOL, OH NO

CHAPTER 11 - WILL THE REAL ME PLEASE STAND UP

CHAPTER 12 - THE INEVITABLE

CHAPTER 13 - THIS IS THE PLAN

CHAPTER 14 - TWO GOOD HIGH SCHOOL THINGS

CHAPTER 15 - DEB GOES TO COLLEGE

CHAPTER 16 - ELTON JOHN GOES TO COLLEGE

CHAPTER 17 - KALENE AND ELTON JOHN

CHAPTER 18 - REALLY BAD THERAPY

CHAPTER 19 - BACK WHERE I STARTED

CHAPTER 20 - THE GREAT ESCAPE

CHAPTER 21 - GETTING OUT OF DODGE

CHAPTER 22 - HOME AT LAST

CHAPTER 23 - VIVA LAS VEGAS

CHAPTER 24 - CARMA MY KARMA

CHAPTER 25 - HELP, I NEED A DOCTOR

CHAPTER 26 - CAN WE TALK?

CHAPTER 27 - 14 GENERATIONS

CHAPTER 28 - HOW I MET COREY

CHAPTER 29 - PRE-WEDDING JITTERS

CHAPTER 30 - LET THE CHURCH BELLS RING

CHAPTER 31 - MY KYLE

CHAPTER 32 - COREY TEACHES ME

CHAPTER 33 - ALYSSA

CHAPTER 34 - ECT ERASE ME

CHAPTER 35 - LATER THAT NIGHT

CHAPTER 36 - HEALING DOESN'T HAPPEN OVER NIGHT

CHAPTER 37 - SING! SING A SONG OF PRAISE

CHAPTER 38 - THE MISSING PIECE

CHAPTER 39 - STILL STANDING STILL TEACHING

CHAPTER 40 - AMAZING GRACE

CHAPTER 41 - I DIDN'T KNOW

EPILOGUE / EMPATHS

ACKNOWLEDGEMENTS

Introduction

I am fascinated with the differences and even more the similarities between religions and their cause. So many times, it has just been a different interpretation of a word or phrase which changed the entire culture of the religion. I have found a richness in being able to combine the commonalities and the differences to deepen my own truth. And… it is in that spirit that I am approaching you…

Originally, when I began this book eight years ago, I was doing it like a research paper and writing more for the women of my specific faith. I was raised with Christian beliefs and values. For years I gathered every scripture every quote every article I could find that would pertain to the things I was writing about. I created an overwhelming bibliography with massive amounts of footnotes. (Actually, the footnotes alone could be their own book.)

I now realize, that research was just for me. What I needed to do, was share my story. There are already many well written research papers and books about this subject. What I have to offer, is my personal take on how to overcome and triumph over adversity. There are though, some specific tenants of my faith that I feel need to be explained to better understand my perspective.

The first tentpole is that the Godhead is made up of God, Jesus Christ, and the Holy Ghost each being distinct separate personages, working together in perfect harmony. God and His Son, Jesus Christ, have perfect, resurrected, glorified bodies of flesh and blood. The Holy Ghost, or Holy Spirit is a personage of spirit only, allowing him to be many places at the same time. But most of all, allowing him to dwell within each of us personally.

Second, I believe that before we came to earth, we lived as spirit children of our loving Heavenly Parents, making us literal sons and daughters of God. This is why I will often refer to God as Heavenly Father or Father in Heaven. While there, in heaven, we wanted to be just like our perfected Heavenly Parents. Thus, we committed to go to earth to gain a body as well as gain all the knowledge and understanding we could. Many lessons would be difficult. However, none would be impossible with the help of our Savior and brother, Jesus Christ.

Third I believe in personal revelation only as it pertains to ourselves or those whom we have stewardship over.

Fourth, I also believe in modern day prophets who receive updated, continuous revelation for all those in the world at this present time.

Finally, and most profoundly, I believe in the Atonement of Jesus Christ. Through this Atonement, all mankind may be saved by obedience to the laws and ordinances of the Gospel of Jesus Christ.

These basics should give you enough background for the drive behind my quest to triumph over trials and bring me to where I am now.

Please note that each chapter will begin with a hymn or church song and end with lyrics sung by Elton John. The reason… well it's in the book title.

Chapter One

Oh Boy! This is Scary

"I will stand, I will not fall
In a world that's weak I will be strong"
- I Will -

My Grandma K and I once had a discussion on how difficult it would be to write our story because it isn't just 'our' story. This makes me think of a poem I stumbled across decades ago and have kept in mind ever since.

How Many Hurt
-The Foreman-

"Suppose" said I, "You chanced to see
A small boy tumble from a tree,
How would you tell that tale to me?"

"Why, Dad," said he, "I'd simply say
I saw a boy get hurt today
And two men carried him away."

"How many injured would there be?"
I asked. "Just one, of course," said he
"The boy who tumbled from the tree."

"No, no" I answered him, "That fall
Which hurt the lad, brought pain to all

Who knew and loved that youngster small"

"His mother wept, his father sighed,
His brothers and his sisters cried,
And all his friends were hurt inside."

Remember this your whole life through
Whatever hurts may come to you
Must hurt all who love you, too."

You cannot live your life alone,
We suffer with your slightest groan,
And make your pain or grief our own."

If you should do one shameful thing,
You could not bear alone the sting,
We'd spend our years in suffering."

"How many hurt, we cannot state,
There never falls a blow of fate,
But countless people feel its weight."

I will try very hard to be general where I can. However, to be honest, accurate, and open, I must reveal the fault of others. For that, I am truly sorry. Currently in my life, I feel nothing but love and compassion for these men. I have not always felt that way, but I honestly do now. I will openly share how this came to be.

Please… please do not stand in judgment. Approach each scenario as if it were your own. You will get so much more out of this. However, I know if you are reading this because you have been abused yourself, it may be hard for you to accept where I am right now. That is completely understandable. It has taken me over forty years to heal.

I think this book may help.

I also will need your compassion. Though I know with all my heart I am supposed to write this story, I am also very queasy about what I am revealing. I feel like I am standing on a stage asked to strip naked. I am about to take off all my clothes to show a body of an overweight 59-year-old woman with sagging skin. With a girdle on, I look great. But even I cringe sometimes when I look in the mirror on the way to the shower.

I promise I will be quite open when required. Still, you must know that this is not easy for me by any means. Candidly, I am quite afraid. I know there will be many who will want to judge me as well. I believe that is why it is so hard to find a personal book about one's own sexual abuse. The victim is as disgusting to many as the abuser. It is hard to understand unless you have lived through it yourself.

I now know a lot of different things I could have done.

It might have been as simple as me just saying stop,

Or getting up and leaving,
Or maybe not…

Therein lies the problem.

You need to understand, and I must keep in mind myself, I was not the same person then, as I am now. I was a little girl first, and then only a youth who had become tainted. That is why, as you read this you will see it really is not a story about how I forgave those who abused me.

This is a story of how I forgave myself.

You see, I think this is the biggest problem for woman, especially those raised in strict religious backgrounds. To forgive yourself you must love yourself as God loves you. That can be very difficult for women holding on to hideous ugly secrets. It has been difficult for me. I had buried the shame of my abuse so deeply that I became consciously unaware of it.

I had been to counseling many, many years with many, many therapists. I have read scores of books on the topic. I have sought spiritual guidance. I have prayed. I have read. I have fasted. I have poured over the scriptures and words of prophets. Through all this, I was able to forgive my abusers as I understood the concept of forgiveness.

But, therein lies the rub. When I forgave them, but still felt the pain, it became more my shame, My fault. The pain of that shame grew to an eventual literal cancer.

I did not understand fully in all my study exactly what the Atonement was capable of, nor did I understand what a single event could do to both the spirit and the body. For me, it was all a cover-up. Yet, it wasn't truly buried. It was growing like worms just under my skin. Every now and then something would trigger the insects and I would see them, and convince - or try to convince myself - that I had already killed them.

They should not be there. The shame deepened. I could not destroy the infestation. A good Christian woman who loved, who forgave and lived the gospel with such vigor should be able to get rid of those unwanted bugs. But they would not go away, no matter how many prayers, or callings or service projects I completed.

That is, not until two days before I began to write this story. I had a vision, and believe me, this is as hard for me to admit as it is for you to read, and maybe even believe.

I will describe some parts of this vision in detail moving forward in this book. Over an eight-year period I experienced the same vision four times. Although it was the same revelation, each time I saw it, I was able to get a better understanding. I also was given a different commandment each time at the end, leading me to this story.

With few exceptions, I will use journal entries from the very first time I experienced the revelation. If I do use a later journal entry, I will identify that.

But for now, I will just say it changed me.

I finally began to understand how all-encompassing the Atonement of Jesus Christ is. I also was taught directly from my Father in Heaven, how to use that Atonement for just an average nobody like me. In all my searching of the gospel I could never find the connection. God was aware of that. So,

He showed it to me. Then, He commanded me to show it to others. So, I am.

As hard as it is to expose myself, I will, because my Heavenly Father and His Son Jesus Christ gave me such a gift and showed me how to use it. For that I am eternally grateful and humbled. I really am not anyone special. Or should I say anyone more special?

I am just a regular wife, a mother to three, who loved to conduct the choir on Sundays.
I have wonderful friends; I try to stay active in my community. I don't have a high-powered job, I'm not a CEO of an organization. I'm not famous, nor have I earned my doctorate degree.

But you know what? No one made a difference until they did. So, I pray with all my heart that in time my stories will make a difference to someone who is searching and needs to feel joy just like I did.

Joy!

That is what I truly feel and what I want everyone to feel. "Man is that he might have joy." I would often read those words in the scriptures or hear them in church. Every time I would try to feel that emotion and it would elude me. I had convinced myself that it really meant joy in the next life. Maybe in mortality, not everyone feels joy. Maybe if I "endured to the end" (one of my least favorite set of words), I would be given joy in heaven.

I couldn't feel joy because of those stupid little bugs creeping throughout my body, those worms. I kept trying to bury, ignore or convince myself they didn't really exist. But they did.

Worse, they were multiplying because that is what bad things do when left unattended. Those unseen insects caused by acts of abuse were eating me alive; both physically and spiritually.

I did not understand it. Others could not put their finger on it. Most people were not even remotely aware I didn't feel joy. I am good at pretending. Most victims are.

A "trigger warning": After telling a bit about my young self, and some background, I will tell of the first event of the sexual abuse that changed me completely. It has only been recently that I have realized how much it altered every part of me and my perception of the world.

I thought I was spiritually damaged, but I did not know that such desecration could meld into my physical being. I hope I can explain what I mean by that as I continue my story…enough stalling - here I go.

> *"And can you feel the love tonight?*
> *How it's laid to rest?*
> *It's enough to make kings and vagabonds*
> *believe the very best."*

God calls me Deb and thank you Elton John

*- Can You
Feel the Love Tonight -*

Chapter 2
My Vision

"The curse of darkness is withdrawn
The Lord from heav'n has spoken"
-The Voice of God Again is Heard-

This is an excerpt from my diary in 2014 immediately following my vision.

The picture He opened inside His scrapbook, which is very similar to the ones I keep, was a picture of me as an eight-year-old girl, who I remembered perfectly. I was sitting on a brick wall of a church building. I had just come out from the day of my baptism.

I was happy. I was filled with joy. I was all the things that I knew I could be at that moment. I knew that what lay ahead of me was everything I could ever want.

I was perfect. I had just been baptized. I had committed no sin, nothing wrong.

My hair was blonde in a high bun like my mother used to do. I had my legs crossed. I felt so grown up. And I had that smile. That incredibly radiant smile.

He then closed the book and let me sit with Him for a minute.

Then He departed.

It is obvious that my spirit was bursting through the limits of my physical body with love and joy and praise for God. I felt as if my Heavenly Father and Mother had a scrapbook, and this was their favorite picture of me. It's so much to describe.

It is interesting to me to read my first take on the vision. I am so grateful I got to experience it three more times, because I missed or misunderstood some crucial parts.

Here's a hint * Pay close attention to my simple understanding of the sentence *"I felt as if my Heavenly Father and Mother had a scrapbook, and this was their favorite picture of me."*

"You, you'll be blessed
You'll have the best
I promise you that."
-Blessed-

Chapter 3
The Girl with Her Hair in a Bun

"I want my life to be as clean as earth right after rain
I want to be the best I can and live with God again"
-When I am Baptized-

I was a perfect example of a child in the 60s becoming an adolescent in the 70s. My family was situated in the nicer middle-class realm of everything material, physical and spiritual.

I had friends. I had fun.

I had blond hair and blue eyes that could change to green if that would better suit an outfit. I was cute but nothing overdone, naturally feminine and compassionate. My world was far from perfect yet, there were no traces of that when I smiled. My eyes would shine with a zest to be great.

I loved and was loved.

I was a huge dreamer. My favorite TV shows were always the award shows. Of course, then, there weren't so many, and they weren't as superfluous. I loved the Academy Awards. I would watch that event with complete conviction that I would someday be on that stage. Throughout the rest of the year, I would practice a speech in the mirror.

My "thank you's" changed as my moods changed. Sometimes, my mom and dad were mentioned, sometimes a teacher, sometimes a sister, but always, I knew at the end of the speech, I would thank my Heavenly Father. I knew that may be a bit controversial, yes even in the 70s. But I also knew where all good things came from.

I pictured myself as a singer. I just knew someday I would grow up and be the next Barbra Streisand. I can't help but chuckle now. My poor neighbors. I would sing in full voice in the backyard for hours. Among my favorite songs were Delta Dawn, Downtown and anything Donny Osmond sang. I would also organize the neighborhood into gigantic music videos (before they were invented, I might add). I would place all of us strategically on our deluxe swing set and have us sing at various intervals. We sounded great. At least I don't remember any stories of the neighborhood complaining and we had so much fun. As I got a little bit older, I did become more aware that there were neighbors and did try to muffle my singing somewhat; however, I always had a tune on my lips. Life was an opera or at least a musical.

I was blessed with an incredible imagination. My bike was a horse that rode like the wind, the fence a balance beam in the Olympics and I was constantly coming up with stories that led my friends and me to really fun games.

My entire world was a stage; a stage where everyone was in the audience and clapped for me with awestruck amazement at my talent.

My pets were never store-bought, and the varieties were astounding. I had a snail farm that had actual families. I made houses and stores for them in a red wagon with sand. I planned on making an entire town for them until one day my younger sister began eating the snails. Totally grossed out, and probably with encouragement from my mother, I got rid of the snails. They were replaced with a caterpillar city.

Eventually, I moved on to mammals. My father brought home a baby kangaroo mouse he had found at work. I would get up faithfully every two hours and feed that tiny thing. I wept when it died. I took it to the hills and gave it a proper funeral. I even wrote a poem about him called "A Single Rose." I am sure I still have that poem somewhere.

Funny how now I can recall just how much I loved to write songs and poems. How had I forgotten that? Some were pretty good, and I received a lot of praise for them. Still, although many teachers would present the idea, I never dreamed of, or even wanted to become a writer (go figure).

I was also extremely perceptive, though I would not understand how much or how that affected the way I saw the world until decades later. I could "read the room" with complete accuracy.

I also thought differently than most people around me. For me, every idea became an analogy that I would recall for any topic. I didn't even know others didn't think the same way.

My love for Jesus Christ was instilled in me from the very beginning; my mother gets the credit for that. She was the strong spiritual influence in our home. I attended all church functions. I never doubted that I was indeed "a child of God" Though later in my life I would have to really explore that concept, I never lost my testimony of Jesus Christ.

These are good memories. Some forgotten until just now. I did have joy then, though I later could not remember how it felt to experience such an emotion.

I did giggle and blush.

I smiled and laughed far more than I hid and cried.

I liked myself, even enjoyed myself.

I had forgotten how much… (how sad).

There was also an undertow in my life. A force of violence lurking just below the surface eventually waiting until conditions were right. I think of it now as a generational meanness. Everything ugly and nasty waiting to surface and touch my foot if I left my socks off.

The violence was there when I was born. My dad had extreme periods of what I would call "darkness." The darkness manifested itself through harsh acts of violence leveled
towards my mom, then me and my siblings. Today, I know the "darkness" was his Depression. There was always fear.

I don't carry horrible negative emotions of my earlier childhood. I am aware of events that should at least trigger sadness; however, I've always been able to look upon those years before I was baptized at age eight and see them for what they were; mostly good with an amount of downright awful just for good measure.

For example, I can clearly call to mind an event that that happened when I was quite young – so young, my favorite shows were Romper Room and Hobo Kelly (compare to Barney or Blue's Clues). My father, after yelling and cursing at her, hit my mother. I remember her head hitting the cupboard behind her in the kitchen. I can hear her pleading with my dad to stop. I was screaming and crying, also asking my dad to stop. There is no emotion or trigger attached to this memory. I can observe the scene, almost clinically. The serious trauma for those periods were completely erased when I was baptized at age eight.

Unfortunately, there are many memories of this nature.

For example, I think about another kitchen years later. Almost the exact chain of events occurred. Only this time it was not just me screaming. I was joined with my two sisters and a brother. A few more years later it would happen all over again, only this time
there were two more sisters to add to the chorus of pleading and crying. These were not the only scenarios.

However, as I look and compare these three instances, even now I was able to tell the first story (pre-baptized) with very little emotion, but I have had to stand up, pace, and grab an extra box of Kleenex to tell the second two. I should have probably put more credence on how baptism erased the insanity before.

Still, I understand and appreciate it now. And while I am grateful to have been raised with strong religious convictions, there has always been a part of me that wishes I could have been baptized four years later.

> *"Here I am for what it's worth*
> *Another well-worn page*
> *But you're all ears so listen up*
> *Hear what I have to say"*
> -Children's Song-

Chapter Four

The Girl with Her Family

"I am a Child of God, and He has sent me here
Has given me an earthly home
with parents kind and dear"
-I Am a Child of God-

I came from a big family. I eventually became the oldest of seven children. My father was the second of eight, my mother was the second of only two. Both sides of the family had yelling, lots of it.

I knew my mother's side did not like my dad. They had some valid reasons for that.
However, I can't help wishing they would have seen the effects their disdain had on me and the rest of the grandchildren. It is hard to be a part of a family where you must feel as if you're picking sides all the time.

Still my Grandma K's house was wonderful and safe. I eventually considered that as my real place to go home. This is where I learned how to be kept safe, and keep others safe, to disagree and even yell but not fight and to see things from another's perspective.

The setting in my father's family was quite different. One thing, there were so many people. Each of his siblings had lots of children as well. Sadly, most of the family get-togethers consisted of the kids playing in the basement as loud as we could to drown out the yelling coming from the brothers upstairs. The mothers would be hiding in a bedroom with their babies. The rides home from these family events were frightening.

Those of us that were older knew not to talk and we would do all we could to keep the younger kids quiet. I love my cousins. I enjoy them. Yet I can freely admit I never looked forward to going to Grandma's house on my dad's side.

> *"So be careful when they're kind to you*
> *Don't you end up in the dirt.*
> *Just remember what I'm saying to you*
> *And you likely won't get hurt."*
> -Son of Your Father-

Chapter Five
Consequence of a Moment

*"Angels above us are silent notes taking
Of every Action, then do what is right."*
-Do What is Right-

I was a little girl, just beginning to blossom into puberty, soon to start my period.

I don't remember any kind of warning or feeling of hesitation the morning I was told to go camping with my dad and two sisters. It was not a first-time event. In fact, the location we were to camp in was one we'd visited before and went to after. Nor can I recall why my whole family wasn't going this time.

I am not sure the preparation it took for me to get ready for the trip. I am sure I must have helped pack clothes and sleeping bags with my sisters. I can't summon up memories for the trip up there. I must have been excited, anticipating sitting around the campfire and roasting marshmallows. I have no memory of the things that took place once we got there. Did we even roast marshmallows?

It must have been fun. I must have really enjoyed the evening being where the stars cluttered the sky of royal blue, a view one can only get in the mountains.

I do remember the army green tent.

I remember the single blowup mattress we were all to sleep on.

I remember there was a camping chair in the corner.

I painfully remember the sound of the zipper as it slid open and shut.

I can recall exactly how my sisters and I giggled about how chilly it was as we changed into our pajamas; how we were looking forward to snuggling into our sleeping bags that had been zipped together to form one big envelope to bury our bodies in for warmth. It is easy for me to conjure up the crisp air, the lingering wave of smoke
from the fire outside. I can hear a little bit of the squealing that only can come from three girls delighted with life as we jostled over our positions in the warmth under the covers.

As I look back on that moment, I've searched for any kind of indication of what was about to happen. I find none.

I had total faith, love and trust for the man who was about to lay next to me.

There was no hesitation to cuddle up with my back towards him.

I was not in any way alarmed as he put his arms around me to hold me closer. I only relished the additional warmth.

Sleep did not come immediately. I was happy and wanted to feel the joy of the camping trip for a bit.

I was aware of the even breathing coming from my sisters as their sleep deepened. Mostly, I felt safe, cozy and peaceful as I began my own descent into dreamland.

Time plays tricks on you when your sleep comes, and that night was no exception.
I can't tell you how long the man waited. I would like to think he must have wrestled with his inner self trying desperately to withstand the abhorrent temptation that invaded his mind. What I would really like to think is that some demonic possession took place.

However, I know that is not the case. I do know that Satan's minions had to be present for such a hideous act. Even now I can still feel the tangible, iniquitous scene as my senses became acute. I did not understand the impression that night. I was later to learn that I was recognizing evil.

I awoke or became cognizant of being touched in a sexual nature.

And kind reader, please allow me to step back a minute. Though my logical mind knows - and I've read countless books… I've been told many times by therapists - I cannot grasp this next particular part.

I have read a great deal about automatic body responses. Yet my heart still, after all I have learned, studied and even after being directly shown by my Heavenly Father, suffers such pain with this part. For when I woke, my body was not just being touched sexually, it was reacting with the pleasure feelings such touch can bring. It was actually the peak of this touch that fully awoke me.

Instant total awareness of the situation immediately overcame me. The utter anguish, shame, and horror of what had taken place entirely consumed me. The safe, cozy and peaceful feeling I had, what seemed to me only seconds before, were stripped from me and thrown so far, I would not be able to find them for over forty years. Though I would search…continuously.

In their place I received the emotions of shame, terror, and betrayal. I cried as silently as I could. My extreme mental distress became overwhelming, and I began to sob.

Then, in that heinous moment, the man I once thought of as a great dad, had the cruel audacity to ask me what was wrong. I was a child for crying out loud! He had to feel the guilt and shame even greater than I did. How could he dare to ask me what was wrong?

It was in that second, I changed entirely. My soul was so offended it literally altered my spirit and my physical body. It affected me at a very cellular level. Of course, I did not and could not understand that piece in that moment. I only just understood it two days before beginning this book - after God showed me.

But I did know then that the world I loved was obliterated.

Yet, so acute was my need to protect the feelings of others, even this sinful man. I lied.
I made up a story right there. I was good at it - I was an actress. I told him about having a nightmare where my family died. I went on to talk about how much I loved them and how afraid I was to live without them. I did everything I could at that moment to protect the abuser who had literally just destroyed the best part of me.

Who does that? As my Heavenly Father showed me in His glorious vision, a loving little girl, that's who…that's who does that.

God's view of the event is so different than what my outcome became…

And I see that now.

But that night, and the years that followed, the worms that would infect me started to grow. They became not just a concept but a reality. I wish I could say this was the only occurrence of abuse with my father. I can say this was the only abuse from him in this way. There would be a great deal of physical abuse; and so much emotional abuse.

However, for the purpose of my story, and because I think this is by far the most significant, even among the violent and inhuman treatment that came later from other abusers…This created the most "Bugs."

I believe it is because this was not just abuse suffered by my body, it was abusive to my spirit. It was also the event of abuse I never told. Never in its entirety until this very moment.

There were other abusers and many violent acts I would fall prey to. There was even a time where I abused myself. I'm not sure any of that would have taken place without this first event. I was very confident and self-assured. No one would have been able to put me in that position if I hadn't first suffered at the hands of my father.

I am experiencing a cleansing in the telling, the survival of admitting - and even compassion for myself.

There is a victory in the ability to share to help another. Most of all, I feel a peace in the fact that I will obey part of an extremely difficult assignment given to me by God to write this chapter.

> *"What do I gotta do to make you love me?*
> *What do I gotta do to be heard?"*
> -Sorry Seems to be The Hardest Word-

Chapter Six
Thank You Elton John

"Be still my soul: The Lord is on thy side
With patience bear thy cross of grief or pain"
-Be Still My Soul-

I will never forget the first day back to class after that
weekend. I made it through the first three periods, just fine.
Got to work. I was a good student so doing my homework in
class was nothing new, nobody paid attention. Eventually,
though it came time to go to the cafeteria.

Immediately I walked to the locker and put all my stuff in it
and just by habit turned around to start facing the lunch
area. As I got closer to the cafeteria, an overwhelming
panic came over me, something I had never experienced
before. It became hard to breathe.

I could see everybody, so many students known and
unknown. I knew that if anyone of them turned their heads
and saw me at that moment, they were going to know
everything that had taken place over the weekend. They
were going to laugh at me.
They were going shame me. I was not going to be able to
handle it.

Somehow my strong legs kept me walking forward. With each step, sounds were becoming more and more muffled. It was becoming harder and harder to breath.
I could see the distance to my table of friends who were waiting for me to get there. No one really acted different. It felt as if I was dragging my feet through the thickest pile of quicksand.

And just when I thought I couldn't do it and was about to drop my lunch and turn around, through the chaos a voice from the radio pierced my mind. At first it just lulled me; I couldn't hear the words. Just the timber of his voice gave me comfort. The more I focused on the voice, the easier it became to breath, the easier it became to let things become more realistic in the cafeteria. Those people weren't really looking at me as I walked to the table.

Everything faded away as I heard the voice on that radio tell me…

"How wonderful life is now you're in the world." And I believed him.

I didn't know at that moment it was Elton John. I wouldn't know that until a week later.
But I knew that this was my guardian angel. I had no doubt.

I was in middle school then, but even now at age 59 I call him my natural Xanax. It's because my whole life, he's not only been my guardian angel by always coming on the radio when I most needed him. He's taught me life lessons. From him, I have learned to appreciate differences and find similarities amongst them. I've watched him change the things he knew he needed to. I've watched him fight for the things important to him. He has always comforted me with music.

A week later I went across the street to a friend's who had an older brother. He was in his room listening to a new Elton John album called Yellow Brick Road and the song that was playing was an instrumental called "Funeral for a Friend." Elton John wasn't even singing yet, but I still knew the comforting feeling. Instantly, all I wanted to do was sit and listen to my guardian angel. And while it might have annoyed my friend a bit, her brother was fine with just letting me sit in the room and escape within that record.

A couple days later I took all my allowance and bought my first album.

> *"I hope you don't mind; I hope you don't mind*
> *That I put down in words*
> *How wonderful life is now you're in the world"*
> -Your Song-

Chapter Seven
My Brutality

"As I have loved you, love one another
By this shall men know ye are my disciple
If ye have love one to another"
-Love One Another-

Recently, I have been reflecting on how a victim could become an abuser, knowing the pain it causes. It is hard to imagine why anyone would want to inflict that kind of suffering on another person. Sadly, when I reflect on the overwhelming emotion of anger and the intense isolation of a dark secret, I can see how it can happen if not addressed.

Immediately after that first abusive encounter I became quite withdrawn. It was easy to hide in my family. I was the oldest. A lot was going on and my dad was pretty much the center of attention when he was home; the youngest, or loudest, when he wasn't. I could hide away for a little bit.

But when I got to school things were different. There was no hiding.

I remember one particular day; I was extra angry with my mom and dad because I had been given a lecture where my dad was quoting scripture. I don't think I comprehended the

word "hypocrite" but looking back that is the word I would
have used.

I was on the playground, and the girls gathered together to
play on the jungle gyms. There was one little girl named
Colleen, and for some reason I got with a group of kids that
were teasing her. They were insisting that she had to stuff
her bra; that there was no way she could be that size. "Hey,
Colleen, can we have a Kleenex?"

It was easy to see that the teasing was getting her very upset.
I'd never participated in something like that before in my
life. I don't even remember considering behaving
intentionally cruel before. She was embarrassed. She was
insisting that she did not stuff.
Somehow, I don't even remember why it got to be me she
would show, but it makes me question, was I was the
meanest or kindest one there? Worse yet, was I the leader of
the bullying? I honestly, don't remember.

What I do know is I was okay with somebody else hurting
the way I was.

We decided we'd go in the bathroom, and I would go into a
stall. She would be in the next stall, and I'd stand on the
toilet, look over the edge and she'd show me whether or not
she stuffed. I remember going in the bathroom and suddenly
feeling awful about it. I still can perfectly picture standing on

the toilet leaning over the edge. I remember seeing just enough to know that she had been honest.

But what I will never forget? What has haunted me for all the rest of my life, was seeing her face. I will never forget that humiliation; that shame, that embarrassment fully exhibited there. I recognized it immediately.

I wished at that moment the world would swallow me up, because I did something very cruel. I don't remember if I was mature enough to apologize at that time. I at least hope… pray that I muttered out a little "I'm sorry."

I do know it was at that moment that I realized that inside me was not just potential for loving, but also the potential for cruelty. Maybe we all have this potential. Maybe depending on how we respond when things that happen in our lives, will be how we define our potential. Will we become bullies? Will our potential be frightening? Will our potential be glorious? Will we overcome?

I've never bullied anyone since then. I hope I never do.

I am grateful in all of my repentance process I haven't been able to forget that one day, that one little girl. I pray with all my heart she will be extra blessed for her suffering. I'm so sorry Colleen. I'm sorry and also very humbled, that God used you to teach me a lesson that lasted a lifetime.

"I've seen a lot of women who haven't had much luck,
I've seen you looking like you've been run down by a truck"
-Dirty Little Girl-

Chapter Eight
Separating Deity

"Our Father, which art in Heaven…
For Thine is the kingdom and the power
And the glory forever…Amen"
-The Lord's Prayer-

After the initial abuse by my father, God had become fractured in my mind. No longer could I associate a father with love. Heavenly or not. I could not do it. But fortunately for me, because of the way our doctrine works, I was temporarily able to separate God/Heavenly Father from God/Jesus Christ. I believe…actually, I know that if weren't for this particular belief I would not have been able to hold onto my faith.

Faith was and has always been my most valuable tool for every aspect of my life. I knew logically that Christ would do nothing contrary to what His Father wanted. I knew He was a complete, perfect example of God the Father. But spiritually and emotionally I knew I could relate to Christ. I knew He loved me and understood me.
He suffered similar things that I seemed to suffer. He was abused and beaten. He had emotional and mental abuse. He often tried to be alone to gather His thoughts. I knew He knew me in a way that no one else could know me and I

loved Him. I still love Him to this day and would give my life for Him.

An example of that love occurred after the turn of the century. I had recently participated in a new surgery. It was an unnecessary surgery that I allowed myself to be pressured into by my doctors. I was the very first one to ever have this procedure done in the state, (at the time that seemed like a real exciting thing, now it seems like a very stupid thing).

I went into that surgery with a third of the information I needed to prepare myself for the potential complications. I came out of the surgery very sick. From that moment on, my room was filled with medical students and doctors. There finally came a time where I was able to be alone in the room with my husband. I was telling him that not only was I feeling sick, but I was in a lot of pain. He stayed until my pain decreased to a manageable level. After he made sure I was comfortable, he went home to be with the kids for the night.

Not 30 minutes after he left, I had a heart attack. I can remember being rushed down the hall. I remember the shouting. Lots of shouting. I remember very quietly saying a prayer, "I'm really scared; I think I'm dying." I flatlined on the table for a short time.

I knew what happened to me. I was immediately enveloped in the arms of Jesus Christ. He didn't say anything, but He did hug me. I will never forget the feeling of being in His arms. It felt warm. It felt safe. It felt complete. After a time, I had to go back. But I returned knowing I would do anything for the rest of my life to fall back into those loving arms. I had never felt love so pure.

I am very grateful I've been able to have such a close relationship with Christ throughout my life. I don't know where I would have been otherwise. I wasn't always an obedient disciple, but I always knew Him and that He loved me.

Unfortunately, as I got older and more things happened, the fracture seemed to become bigger and bigger. Again, let me state, I was taught and believed that Christ did nothing that was contrary to the will of His Father. Still, I felt that God was mean. And that Christ was the loving one.

And though I had my beautiful relationship with Christ, I wanted more than anything to feel that way about His Father. I wanted to feel His love and the fact that I couldn't, made me feel more shame. It was very hard for me not to think that some of the things that were happening to me were because of a mean God. How could I possibly understand the concept of a father that was loving?

As I grew, I could see others did feel God was loving. That was not hard for me to justify. My dad treated people, especially his children differently.

It still hurt and deepened my shame. I knew God was perfect, so the fact that there was something wrong with my relationship with Him, or at least it felt to me like there was something wrong made me feel even worse about myself because I was unable to fix it.

(Okay, I'm stepping out of my story for a minute. I want to make this point very… very… clear. Fathers…know that your example to your children will determine the way they see God. I'm not implying that like me, they can't work to find their own understanding. However, I firmly believe you, as a father or parent, will be held responsible for creating such a misrepresentation of who God is.)

I never believed that God the Father didn't love me. Quite the opposite - I knew He did. That had nothing to do with whether He was mean or not. I think these are two truths seeming almost contradictory, that an abused child can hold. They believe their dad loves them. But they are also scared to death of him and try to avoid all interaction with him. And then it gets even more confusing because there is also an innate drive to try to get their dad's approval.

And that's the relationship that I developed with God because I didn't know any better. The men I saw, at least when away from church, were the same kind; they were angry.
It was very hard for me to see it any differently.

> *"If there's a God in Heaven What's He waiting for…*
> *But It seems to me that he leads His lambs*
> *To the slaughterhouse and not the promised Land"*
> -If There's a God in Heaven-

Chapter Nine
The Grooming

"Here bring your wounded hearts,
Here tell your anguish
Earth has no sorrow that heaven cannot heal"
-Come, Ye Disconsolate-

It wasn't too much later that I had an uncle begin the "Grooming Process" with me. Of course, back then I don't think that term even existed. It began when I was 12 or 13 years old.

By this time, we lived in a good-size two story house. It had a big empty formal dining room. The only thing in it was a one-piece mirror that covered the entire wall. (I clearly remember my dad always emphasizing that it was one-piece.)

The room was great for practicing dance routines, preparing for plays and vocal competitions. I remember one year me and a very good friend of mine dressed up as Raggedy Ann and Andy. (Should I be embarrassed that 50 years later I still have that costume?) We made them ourselves. The two of us choreographed a fun dance routine that won not only first place in the school talent show, but also in the regional church talent show. I didn't know that fun routines could become so tainted.

My dad's youngest brother came to stay with us for weeks at a time. I was too young to really know all of his issues. I knew he had been shot in a robbery, though I wouldn't know until years later that he was the robber. I think I had probably heard my parents talk about a drug problem, but I knew nothing about drugs at that age.

To me, Uncle Keith was the coolest thing ever. That's all I knew. It felt like I was hanging with a high school senior. That was awesome to a middle school girl. He taught me to play the guitar in that room. He'd have us look at ourselves in the mirror as we practiced. He started by making comments about how I was going to turn all the boy's heads. What girl doesn't like to hear that?

It is interesting that I wasn't able to pick up on his actual intentions. I know by this time I had begun to really be aware of people's motives. I had been born with a gift to feel the emotions of others. By this time, I had started to develop that talent. The only reason I can think of would have been because it was an emotion or energy I hadn't conceptualized yet.

For example, I remember a next-door neighbor boy who was in high school saying some of the same things to me that my uncle had. There is still a particular song that I can't listen to because that boy would say some of the lyrics to me. I was able to recognize his intentions immediately.

It bothers me that I was so clueless to Keith's motives. Maybe it had something to do with him being family. I'm sure his skills at manipulation were far more advanced than my empathic abilities at that time. He definitely had the "hippie" vibe that resonated with me.

His compliments became more sexual with each visit. The first touches were done as he taught me some of "the more difficult chords" on the guitar. He would stand or sit behind me with his arms coming around me. At first, he would act as if the caresses were accidents, then just natural.

One specific time as we sat on the floor, as had become his custom, he would rest his hands on my thighs between the chords I couldn't quite master. As he moved his hands closer to my crotch I did try to get up. Keith assured me that there were no sexual feelings. I was his niece. He said that I would have to get used to being touched everywhere because dancers and actors had to touch and be touched all the time. That seemed credible to me. I wanted to be a performer more than anything. I was definitely uncomfortable, but I sat there in front of that mirror continuing to try to play that song while he touched me. Afterall, he was helping me master my artistic craft.

But I hated it. I think I actually started hating him too. However, I knew that was not allowed because he was family. I did stop the guitar lessons with him. Fortunately, something happened soon after that evening and he went to stay somewhere else. Unfortunately, it was to prey on others.

I would see him on and off over the next couple years. I had pre-planned excuses to avoid him. Yet his timing was always so good, for him anyway. He would get me alone. It was our secret, and I was his favorite niece. Then he would say how he wished we could be together because we would be so good. I didn't know what he meant by that when I first heard him say that.

Fast forward years later when I was completely broken, Keith was there to get me and my friends' alcohol. Eventually he was giving me minor drugs. I just needed to stop feeling because by then all I felt was pain. I hid that fact. I was the consummate actor after all. Even as I tell this now, I feel nothing but anguish over that time. His abilities to manipulate scare me as I look back. I was not dumb and as I was older, I was far from naïve. I really can't comprehend so much of it.

Looking back, I know that part of the reason Keith was able to get away with so much for so long was because I was in my own self-abuse phase. It wasn't until he had me try to "recruit" other family members that I was able to get out from his clutches. By that time, I hated him as much as I loathed myself.

Many years later, I believe it was the first year I was married, Keith called me very late one night. He began the same old song. I was "his favorite niece" blah blah blah. It was very different this time because I could reach over and touch my husband (actually, by a couple sentences in, Corey was up with his arms around me.) I was able to tell him I wanted nothing to do with him. He was an abuser. I would no longer be his victim.

Within the next two days I would be notified that my Uncle Keith died of an 'accidental' overdose of heroin that night. I have and still do refuse to feel an iota of guilt for that.

Excerpt From The Vision
12/3/14

"I was forced to examine events in my life that have caused me terrible anguish. Some I hadn't even thought about for years. It was like a movie I was being forced to watch, then pushed into living the part, then pulled back out to rewatch until I could finally see things the way my Father in Heaven saw them. I was required to do this same experience; watch over and over until I got it right before I could move onto the next experience. Some of the events only needed to be viewed once; others over and over until I got it right.

Time was suspended but the process seemed long, painful and exhausting. Then the relief and joy would come as I moved through the events. Most of the time I was innocent when I felt guilty, except for once and I will do what I can to make it right.

But each time I could not move on until I felt nothing but love for the little girl (me), myself and the decision, and miraculously, compassion or an understanding for the abuser.

Throughout the process I kept flashing back to a picture of me on the day I was baptized. I was sitting on a church wall in a blue dress with white polka-dots…"

After the second time I experienced the vision, I realized that each time I was becoming overwhelmed or was having a hard time moving on to the next scene, that picture would flash in my mind until I was able to feel calm, patient and ready to continue.

In each vision it felt like this incestuous relationship was the most difficult for me to view it in the same way God viewed it. I had learned the difference between sin and response on an intellectual level. It was extremely difficult for me to sort each of my actions into its correct category. It wasn't until the third time I experienced this vision that I was able to really comprehend the reason I was having such a cognitive dissonance with what God was showing me. I don't think I actually spoke out loud, but my question was "I think I'm mixed up? There is too much in the response category. I'm not supposed to feel remorse or pain for all this stuff?" The response was, "Yes Deb, Exactly."

"But these cuts I have
Oh, they need Love
To help them heal."
-Don't Let the Sun Go Down on Me-

Chapter Ten
High School, Oh No!

"Hallelujah! What a Savior! Hallelujah! What a Friend
Saving, helping, keeping, loving, He is with me to the end."
-Jesus! What a Friend for Sinners-

High School became a very difficult time for me. Where I
once absolutely loved school and everything that had to do
with learning, I began receding further and further from that
kind of environment. I still was able to maintain good
grades. In my whole high school career, I think I had only
two Cs from the same teacher. Both times it was just a
horrible event.

We moved at the end of my freshman year. Losing my huge
group of friends when we left California was devastating.
Though no one in my circle of friends was perfect, we had
the same standards, allowing us to encourage each other,
knowing we were all trying. It wasn't too many years later, I
realized how fortunate I was because I would not find that
in my new High School.

Living in a small town was a different experience for me. I
had a really hard time fitting in. I was not unpopular at
school. I had friends. I had boyfriends that were regular
boyfriends. I was on the tennis team, pep squad, yearbook
committee and music. There was no swim team. I was also

involved in any theater I could find, the small town offered little opportunity. Theater always resonated with me, because it allowed me to escape who I was and be somebody else.

In opposition to that creative side, I was also extremely good at math. I loved the orderliness and concreteness of it. Those were the two things that I enjoyed in my life.

As far as boyfriends, I had my heart broken many times; I went to the proms and homecoming dances. But the older I got, the harder it got to find boys with my morals and standards.

I wanted to fit in. I began drinking. I liked the way it felt. I loved the sensation after the first sip. I didn't like being drunk. I didn't like anything about drinking except that first feeling of having my shoulders relax and feeling like things were going to be okay. And for the rest of the night, I would be chasing that first feeling. But that was dangerous. Especially for a broken high school girl. I learned that a little too late.

My first time getting very drunk was with a couple of football players on a double date. We went to the movies to see the latest James Bond film. After the movie they took us back to someone's apartment. The other girl I was with was lucky to be drunk enough to pass out. So, that just left me. I was too drunk. I couldn't defend myself.

I lost something I had been trying to hold on to. They stole my virginity. It was a violent, painful act. Yet there is a piece of me that still holds a little bit of responsibility because I knew better than to drink. I knew better than to get myself involved in that situation. I should not have been drinking.

And I know right now, that is not politically correct. I should have no fault because I said "No!" Boy did I ever say "No!" But I disagree with the current thinking. I do think I have some fault in that because I was drinking. I should not have been drinking. I was under the age of 21.

A consequence of a mean God? If so, it was going to get a lot worse.

> *"The roar of fire rings on high*
> *The flames light up the black night sky*
> *A child screams out in fear*
> *A hopeless cry for help but no one is near enough to hear"*
> -Madness-

Chapter Eleven
Will the Real Me Please Stand Up?

"Who's on the Lord's side who?
Now is the time to show
We ask it fearlessly, who's on the Lord's side who?'
-Who's on the Lord's Side? -

After the violent act of rape, the boys went back to the locker room the following week and bragged all about it. I don't know the exact story they told. I do know that I was then looked on as a slut. I attended a pretty small high school, so word got around fast.

This was when I broke apart completely. I created different faces, or characters for each situation I was in. At school I kept my head down and focused on my classes. I was friendly but stopped attempting to make friends or even keep most of my close friends.

At church, I was all smiles and participated in choirs, gave solo's and attended most of the activities.

I appeared very professional at my various jobs.

At home I would hide away in my room. I shed lots of tears.

When out in public, like a store or restaurant, I would summon up one of the actresses of a role I recently viewed. Thus, often it was a toss-up as to who the person I was with, was going to get. (In fairness to me, this did lead to some interesting dates, however unfair it may have been to the guy I was with.)

As I got older, I defined the different characters very distinctly. There is a book I recently read by Stephen King called "If It Bleeds." In the description on one of the stories the cover jacket states that King "explores beautifully how each of us contains multitudes." I couldn't agree more.

The problem it caused with me, was that I kept them so separated. Thus, no one really got to know me. They may have thought they did and were not completely wrong because they did know that particular piece of me. After all, I was genuine in the parts of me I showed each group. Still, I associated with a lot of groups in various ways. I was a genius in how I could keep each presentation of myself straight. However, it was so very exhausting. And oh, it was so very lonely

The danger came as I kept reinforcing my internal belief of "Sure they like me and think I'm a good person, but if they knew the 'real' me, or this particular part of me, they wouldn't even want to know me." That is such a hard way to view the world.

Even now, as I'm writing this, I've had to step away a couple times to cry, pray for comfort and finally make my husband (who definitely knows all sides of my characters,) come in and hold me as I sobbed. I'm realizing that I still have that very same fear. How will people feel about me when they hear my whole story?

I am in a place where I will not let that fear paralyze me. As Corey held me, he reminded me that those who do know all of me, and until this story gets out there are only three people, are those who love me the most. So, I will draw on them for courage.
I will continue to reveal it all because God commanded me to. Ultimately, God, who saw it all, was who I feared disappointing the most. Surely, He was as disgusted with the whole of me, as I was. (Spoiler Alert: I couldn't have been more wrong.)

However, at the time His punishments for my sins seemed to be very public and were quite harsh compared with what I knew of those around me. It was that image of a mean God.

> *"Blue eyes holding back the tears, holding back the pain*
> *Blue eyes, baby's got blue eyes, and she's alone again"*
> -Blue Eyes-

Chapter Twelve
The Inevitable

"Till our dreams are rich with meaning
each endeavor, Thy design
Great Creator, lead us onward
'till our work is one with thine."
-Teach Us What We Yet May Be-

Of course, with the whole school thinking I was already a slut, dating became increasingly difficult. Between the guy's insistence that I put out for someone else, so why not him and his declaring false intentions of falling in love with me, it was difficult for me to navigate it all.

Add in my increasing need to feel numb and only knowing how to do that with alcohol and marijuana: plus, my almost non-existent self-worth. Finally, mixing in my religious beliefs, which I still held so dear. I kept convincing myself that something like that would never happen again. The next several years of my life seemed inevitable.

The following is a journal entry from a week before I graduated from High School.

Journal Entry May 27

"On May 12 the doctor told me I was pregnant. I suppose I was as shocked as he was. I always had that fear ever since Dec 14. I had been to a lot of doctors about my head and my heart (due to an auto accident), and no one knew.

I tried to just think that I was being silly. I hoped that if I just never thought about it or did anything about it, it would go away.

But on May 12 I was in for a physical. As the doctor and I talked, I told him about the problems I was having; irregular periods and dizziness; weight gain and often nausea, he assured me that was somewhat normal for a girl in high school especially with so much stress. He was our
small-town family doctor.

Then after having me lay on the table and he felt my stomach, that was it!

He sat down and asked me, "What are the chances that you are pregnant?"

I was numb. I said I could be and that was it. He started to figure out the due date…

…I couldn't believe it. What I feared most was taking place. The doctor asked about my plans.

Plans?! I never made any. I couldn't get married (the guy had dumped me pretty soon after he got what he wanted).

Abortion was out of the question, adoption, yes maybe.

But how could I tell my parents?!

And why me?!!!

I started crying. I wanted to scream and wake up to find it was a nightmare. I left the office in shock.

What would I tell people and most of all I knew my parents would be so hurt…

… I got home, and Mom was in the kitchen. What could I say? She knew something was wrong. I asked her to come to my room. I heard her ask if I wrecked the car.

Oh, how I wish that was all that I wrecked.

When I got to my room I said, "I'm pregnant." The words seemed so unreal. Mom just stood there. She was too numb to say anything. She hugged me but I think it was from lack of believing.

Then Dad came home. Mom talked to him first. I stayed in my room.

I still cry when I think of the time, I waited for Dad to come downstairs. I tried to clean my room, but it was useless. I couldn't see through the tears.

When my Dad came in, I was sick. I mean I totally hated myself. He was so hurt, and I couldn't face him.

He said, "Turn around. You're going to have to face me sooner or later." And when I did, he grabbed me and hugged me. Can you believe it?

Here I was, a total failure, risking not only my happiness, but the whole family as well and he said, "I still love you. Nothing can change that."

We stood that way for a long time not saying anything else; both of us crying.

He didn't know what to do so he and my mom went to talk to our church leader that very night. And me, well I just cried all night till I fell asleep and then woke up and cried some more.

I suppose all I thought was why me; why now?

I was quitting drinking and I already had talked to our clergyman about relationships with guys.

Why? I already started repenting.

So why did this happen to me?

Maybe I still wonder why."

I want to point out how Christlike my dad's reaction towards me was at that moment. Though rare, I'll admit, this was not an isolated incident. My dad did come through in a big way on a few occasions. His behavior did instill in me the quest to understand what a good person was versus a bad person. I don't have an answer to that. I am grateful to know that is not my job. Only God can judge.

While there would come a time when I would have to cut off all contact with my father to enable my healing, I would not refer to him as an evil man, weak in many respects yes, at least as my father, but not completely evil.

> *"Don't wish it away don't look at it like it's forever*
> *Between you and me, I can honestly say that things can only get better"*
> -I Guess That's Why They Call it the Blues-

Chapter Thirteen
This is the Plan

"May I hear thee say to me
'Fear not; I will pilot thee."
-Jesus, Savior, Pilot Me-

It was decided I would put that child up for adoption. And that would be the end of it.

Perhaps, if I knew what I would find out years later, I might have seen the way the situation played out differently. But what I saw were parents that were extremely ashamed of me, who didn't want to do anything but hide me. Parents I discouraged and let down. Before I even knew what was happening, I was being moved to another city with people I didn't know, to live out the entirety of my pregnancy, so I could come home and never talk about it again.

I was to tell no one. I didn't really see a different way and I'm not sure whether that was the best or worst idea. Maybe that was the best thing for me.

The home I was originally placed in was far less than ideal. I was then taken in by another family. I'm sure many would have thought them to be less than ideal. But I loved them. They had the same family dynamics that I had grown up with. I am so grateful for them allowing me to be a part of their family and for the women who befriended me then.

I have to believe it was definitely the best thing for the baby. But I still feel I didn't get a choice.

I actually graduated from high school six and a half months pregnant with honors and a scholarship award for high achievement in math.

I lived in constant fear that someone would find out. Unfortunately, some family members and even the father of the baby was not as discreet as they should have been. People I knew found out anyway.

I was sent away. I had my baby. I signed papers and I came back. And I was never able to mention her again. I went to college. And I tried to forget.

This makes me think of a scripture where Christ asks the rhetorical question about whether a mother could forget her child. He then responds with yes. But He would never forget because we are engraved in the palms of his hands. While I fully appreciate the point Jesus was making, I have found the scripture a bit puzzling. How could a mother forget? I tried and could never forget. I would eventually learn how to grieve such a loss and put the pain in perspective. Forget? Never.

I do have pictures of her and I made her a blanket and I made myself a miniature version of it.

I had this dream of someday being in church and a woman would walk in holding a baby wrapped in that blanket. Because the type of yarn I used and the way I crocheted it was distinct, I would recognize it immediately. It was a very pretty baby blanket. I thought maybe she would come in and she'd have her child wrapped in the blanket and she'd proceed to tell me a story that she was adopted, and that blanket was made by her birth mother. Now she uses it on her baby. And I would know.

I wonder in these modern times if it's best to look her up. I don't know the answer. I truly believe that she was meant for the family she went to. I'm not sure I could help her anyway. So far, I haven't.

> *"Why's it never light on my lawn*
> *Why does it rain and*
> *never say good day to the newborn?*
> -Grey Seal-

Chapter Fourteen
Two Good High School Things

"I need Thee, O I need Thee,
Every hour I need Thee"
-I Need Thee Every Hour-

As I had said before, my life began to be increasingly tough when I moved to a small town at the end of my freshman year. There were two good things that came out of my little high school. Both are blessings that I still treasure.

The first was my continued relationship with Elton John. The amazing thing was the number of times, especially after I learned to drive, that things would just be going so horrible and as I would start up the car, Elton John would be playing on the radio, instantly comforting me; letting me know it was going to be okay. Yes, he was even on the radio when I got in the car after that dreadful doctor's appointment singing "Tiny Dancer." He was everything a guardian angel was supposed to be, always there
whenever I needed him.

At the same time, Elton John seemed to be on every popular form of media. Though I wasn't one to pay a lot of attention to that, I was aware of his willingness to be different.

My mom and dad focused on the things he was doing contradictory to our religious beliefs. They attempted to discourage my admiration. That was never going to happen.

As I heard and saw the things that were printed about him - doing drugs, extreme outbursts, overt sexuality and over the top behavior, it never occurred to me to think about him differently other than that he was my guardian angel. It never changed the way I felt about him. And learning to accept him that way, seeing only the good, I was able to learn to see everyone that way - well everyone except myself. That was a tremendous gift to learn in high school.

The second treasure was my friendship with Wayne. It would only be years later that I would appreciate how important this relationship was. From him I was able to learn to be able to share real feelings and emotions with the person of the opposite sex without sexuality. I also learned that there were men who would never force me to do something that I was uncomfortable with, who would not even be comfortable themselves forcing me to do something I was uncomfortable with. Men who would not become angry when asked to please stop. Oh, how I appreciate that now. He taught me being a man did not mean being an abuser. That was a very important lesson.

It is frightening to think of the marriage, probably marriage(s) I would have suffered through if I hadn't learned from Wayne some of the traits men could have. I was able to recognize those traits in my one and only husband for over 31 years now. Wayne is still one of my best friends. I guess now it is more like he is my big brother. He has helped me talk and work through many difficult matters.

Funny as I think about it now, Wayne and Elton John could not be more different. But without both, I don't think I would have made it. I definitely would not be in the place I am now. Thank you and I love you both.

> *"The great sequin cowboy who sings of the plains*
> *Of roundups and rustlers and home on the range.*
> *Turn on the TV and shut off the lights*
> *Roy Rogers is riding tonight"*
> -Roy Rogers-

Chapter Fifteen
Deb Goes to College

"I pray You'll be our guide and watch us where we go
And help us to be wise in times when we don't know"
-The Prayer-

Finally, I made it to college. I went to Brigham Young University in Provo, Utah. When I first moved there, I lived in the dorms. That was an ideal way to meet people. I shared a room with a young lady that spoke zero English when she arrived. By the end of the semester, we could speak in broken sentences.

There were a lot of really good times, and I am grateful that I got that opportunity. I think the greatest blessing for me was that I knew no one, which allowed me to be a knew character without the old baggage - at least that anyone else could see.

I learned from some fantastic teachers and professors. Many of the lessons were not just scholarly, but lessons that I was able to apply for the rest of my life. Oh, and there were so many possibilities. I got teary-eyed the first time I got to the Theater department. It seemed my dreams were coming true. I absolutely loved the feeling of walking on campus with all the energy of learning. I still do. I bent down to just touch the grass knowing people had studied and received

new ideas there. I relished the opportunity to share new
thoughts with fellow students and get their take.

I loved being in the libraries where so much knowledge was
available. (This was
long before we held libraries on our phones that fit in our
palms.) I cherished (still do) all that had to do with holding
books while walking across campus and…all things college.

School had its hardships. I had to work full time while
attending school. This was a lot different than many of my
friends and roommates who only had to go to school. Many
students worked only part time. Keeping up with my
schoolwork was difficult; my first two semesters I took 15
credit hours, but I still had time to have fun.

I got my job working in a cafeteria along a cafeteria food
line. I began first as a dishwasher which was fairly gross.
When the trays would come in, we would wash them off. I
probably will never forget the smell of that dishwasher. And
later, I got to move out of the kitchen onto the serving line.
That was a blessing in so many ways. One of the biggest
ways was we were able to sneak a little bit of food off the
lines and it helped supplement a little bit of my food bill.

Eventually I moved off campus and lived in an apartment.
We had three bedrooms and one bathroom for six girls that
we paid an outrageous amount of money for even at that

time. It's weird because I can't remember ever fighting over the bathroom.

I had some wonderful, wonderful times there. My roommates and I threw some really fun parties, with absolutely no alcohol or drugs. We even brought sand in for a big beach party and made palm fronds to put on all the lights.

> *"When she gets up in the morning it's enough to raise the dead*
> *She turns on the radio and dances on my head."*
> -Jamaica Jerk Off-

Chapter Sixteen
Elton John Goes to College

"I pray we'll find your light and hold it in our hearts
When stars go out each night, remind us where you are"
-The Prayer-

It should be no surprise that Elton John featured a big part of my college experience as well, sometimes in silly ways.

I had one particular roommate, Darlene, whose favorite singer was Mick Jagger. We used to play Skipbo, our favorite card game. I would have Elton John be my partner (because it's only fun when you play four hands) and she would have Mick Jagger be her partner. Any time I won I was able to say that "the sugar bear got her under her thumb" (for all you rock fans).

I also had another roommate who worked at a clothing store. It was no secret to my friends about how much I loved Elton John. One day my roommate came home so excited. She said, "How much do you want to see Elton John?" and I was like,
"Ah A Lot! I would love to see him!" Up until that point I hadn't been able to see him live in concert. He was playing at the Salt Palace in Salt Lake City. She said, "Well these guys came into the store. They're not much to look at and you're not gonna like them, but they have these tickets to the

Elton John Concert! I told them I had a roommate and that we would love to go." I was completely up for it. Of course, at that time I didn't have any worries about driving to a place an hour and a half away with two guys that we never met. But I was with a roommate, and it was going to be fun.

When we got to the concert our seats were in the very, very top row just under a speaker, I was beyond excited. I could not have cared less about the guy I was with (which was extremely unfair and unkind to him), but whatever, guys have been extremely unfair and unkind to me (not that he deserved it). My roommate and I were sitting in the middle, the two guys flanked us on each end. Eventually, it seemed like forever at the time, the concert started.

Elton John came out. That particular night he had on his clown costume. I remember he opened with "Funeral for a Friend", which instantly resonated with me. It was so loud under that speaker. It was so beautiful and so encompassing. We sat back and began to
listen.

Though the guys with us were getting stoned, I just wanted the music. I knew the only thing I really needed was Elton John's music and it was taking me away to another place. I recall the keyboardist started with some really awesome tones, the intro to "Rocket Man." The song started to take me to a whole other level. I leaned over and put my elbows on my knees, just kind of put my head in my hands so that I could shut out the other feelings and focused only on the music.

The music started to literally inhabit me (I'm sure I was helped because of the nearness of the speaker), my toes began to vibrate, and the feeling started moving up, all the way up. The feeling started shooting out my hair, my fingertips. Every part of me was vibrating. A pleasure so intense; I never imagined my body was able to experience such a sensation. It was one I wouldn't experience again for many years. When the song was over the guy patted me on the shoulder and I leaned up and thought "Holy cow! Does everyone know what just happened to me?" Looking around I saw that no one was the wiser.

On the way home I was sitting as close as I could to the passenger side door and my date kept saying "Hey is the weather different over there?" . . . trying to drop all these hints, but I all I could think was "Hmmm, there is nothing you can do after what Elton John just did for me."

Until that point, I didn't know that kind of feeling could exist. Nor would I know of that feeling again until I was able to discover what making love really meant. And what a sexual relationship really did mean when it was with a person you loved and trusted.
(In fact, that has always been a running joke with my husband and I.)

So, in that moment, Elton John even taught me what joy my body was going to be capable of feeling. And that's crazy. But it's true. He let me know what to aim for.

Now, I've been to many concerts of his since that first one, and many times tried to duplicate that sensation; and while I have been able to have his music inhabit me, I've never been able to recreate that experience. And that's okay, because now I get it from where it should come from. I'm grateful for that lesson. I always had this dream of meeting Elton John in person, and after the initial shock (me weeping uncontrollably and being able to just blubber out the words, "thank you"), I would be able to share that story with him. I'm sure he'd find it funny, and we'd laugh.

> *"Mars ain't the kind of place to raise your kids*
> *In fact, it's cold as hell*
> *And there's no one there to raise them if you did".*
> -Rocket Man-

Chapter Seventeen
Kalene and Elton John

"Let this be our prayer
When shadows fill our day"
-The Prayer-

There was a time when I was driving back to Provo, talking with my dear friend, Kalene, another friend I've kept for life. It had been a particularly difficult weekend for us, and we began to talk about the poor decisions we had recently made and the consequences that would be sure to follow.

My stomach sank as I realized that one of the consequences would be that my only confidant would no longer be going to school with me. I wouldn't get to see her as much. Kalene was my roommate, was like my sister. She was the first I let see most of my true character; now she'd have to move away. I hadn't shared everything about my life (I wasn't even consciously sharing it with myself) but she knew my struggles. I was losing the one person I could be myself with.

She knew that I was striving to be this one person as I struggled with myself, feeling like I was another. And so, it was very hard for me to know she wasn't going to be around -because I pretended a lot in those days. Oh, man, I pretended a lot.

I hate to call it pretending because it wasn't really pretending at the time. I was trying to be the person I wanted to be. I was that person, but it was only a part of who I was. And because I didn't acknowledge the other sides of me, or that other side of me that kept receiving messages that I was even worse than I thought, it felt like pretending.

Though she hadn't actually said I'm no longer going to be your roommate, I remember feeling devastated. But at that moment on the radio this unfamiliar song came on. The voice was in an uncommon register, but I instantly recognized it. "Of course, Elton John is here to comfort me." Kalene said, "That's not Elton John." But it was and I knew it. It was "Blue Eyes," one of the few songs where he starts singing in a very low register. "Yes, it is." To prove what I already knew, we waited until the song ended. The radio announcer confirmed that it was a new Elton John song.

Once again, he was there to comfort me. He was like that. He was always like that.

"Blue eyes, baby's got blue eyes
When the morning comes
I'll be far away."
-Blue Eyes-

Chapter Eighteen
Really Bad Therapy

"Oh Lord, lead us to a place
Guide us with Your grace
Give us faith so we'll be safe."
-The Prayer-

The undercurrent within me during that time was a little bit different. I guess I hoped somehow miraculously I would get to college, and everything would be different. I would have forgotten everything that went on in high school. I would be able to become that new person; that person I was meant to be, that all the rest would go away.

It didn't. No one told me I was grieving. It had only been a couple months since I had lost a little girl. No one had told me that because I had to go through this terribly difficult, huge consequence for something I did, that I knew so many others did, that I would probably carry a bit of resentment for that. Nobody had told me.

Nobody told me that I would still feel as if I didn't fit in; that I would still feel like an outsider, not a part of anything. And there was still my belief that no matter how good of friends I made. if they really knew me, they wouldn't be my friends anymore.

It was suggested by one of my professors to go see a counselor. That felt a little bit tricky during that time to talk with a BYU counselor because they had an honor code. It became a case of what I should share because maybe some of what I would say, I feared may get me expelled because it went against the honor code. I was assured I could say anything, it was all confidential. Even still, it took a couple of meetings to even get the courage to share my real problem.

But this particular counselor, by the second meeting, who really had heard such superficial things about me, determined that I was suffering from a condition he called "Self-defeating Behavior." I don't know if he wrote the workbook on it. I don't know if the workbook was written by a team of BYU professors there at the time. He proceeded to tell me the problem I was having was, instead of doing the best for myself, allowing myself to progress and grow, I was doing behaviors that were actually defeating myself; preventing myself from becoming the person I wanted to be. I didn't argue with that. I was definitely doing some behaviors that were probably defeating. Not once did we take time to explore why I might be doing those behaviors. Or what those behaviors might be representing. Why I chose those behaviors over others? And why I was able to continue to do other behaviors that were very healthy, that were the opposite of defeating; that were ennobling consistently at the same time.

Why one, didn't ever cancel out the other? Why even the good stuff, even though it was probably doubled, no, tripled compared to the bad didn't seem to diminish that in any way.

So again, my experience became to internalize it. The shame was mine. The reason I was falling apart had nothing to do with the things that were done to me. The reason I was falling apart was because now, I was doing things to myself. I had become my own abuser. It was all my fault.

How does a young woman deal with that?

(Stepping out of this story for a minute. I am angry with that counselor. That was utter BS. Shame on therapists who are less about listening than they are about pushing their diagnoses. Believe me, I know there are a lot who do this.)

Eventually it became too much. I couldn't keep myself together.

> *"I think I'm gonna kill myself*
> *cause a little suicide*
> *Stick around for a couple of days*
> *What a scandal if I died"*
> -I Think I'm Gonna Kill Myself-

Chapter Nineteen
Back Where I Started

"Though tribulation rage abroad
Christ says, 'In me ye shall have peace."
-Though Deepening Trials-

I decided to go back to the only place I knew to go - back home. It was very shortly, maybe within a couple weeks, that I had a job and found a place to live. Unfortunately, I got back in with friends that I had left who never did judge me. Probably because most had very few morals. They definitely did not have my best interest at heart.

Worst of all, by that time, my uncle had moved there. As I mentioned earlier, his timing once again was perfect, and he was the very first to swoop in and take me down the rest of my descent. However now it had stopped being just about him. It became about those around him; always in the end pulling me away to show them that I was his not theirs. I don't remember ever enjoying anything or doing anything that made me happy. Most the time. I felt nauseated and disgusting.

For me life became about the escape. What kind of drugs did that the best? How much alcohol and what kind of alcohol? I never did, what I would refer to as hard drugs, though I had many opportunities. I did discover Xanax. My family doctor prescribed it with no questions asked. I started experimenting with mixing the two. That was all I thought about. I learned to manage to escape very well. I remained a hard-working employee. My Church character was genuine on Sunday. I learned to use that escape everywhere I went; everything I did. But I couldn't keep that pace forever. With the lifestyle I was living things began to fall apart.

The person I was dating at the time began to lose interest. (Rightly so because I was a mess.) But I did love him… and so more pain. My supposedly "best friend" ended up sleeping with him. That really hurt because I had been propositioned so many times by her boyfriends throughout high school and when I returned. I would never do that to her. The night I found that out, feeling so betrayed, I again needed to escape the only way I knew. I went to a party. The stupidest thing I could do because it was with people I didn't know well.

I tried to be safe, because I didn't know hardly any of them, except for the person throwing the party and I only knew him from a few interactions at work. I knew it would be stupid to drink too much, so I kept my drinking to a minimum. I think I only had one beer. But that was before I knew anything about doses being added to drinks. I don't know if that was even very common. Maybe people just didn't talk about it. Either way I didn't know to watch for that. I don't want to say too much about the evening, I can only think of it with flashes. But it was bad.

It wasn't too much later that I realized again, I was pregnant.

Of course, I thought God was mean.

> *"I'm looking for the dolly who will see me right*
> *I may use a little muscle to get what I need"*
> -Saturday Night's Alright for Fighting-

Chapter Twenty
The Great Escape

"Oh, may my soul commune with thee, and find thy holy peace
From worldly care and pain of fear, please bring me sweet release."
-Oh, May My Soul Commune with Thee-

When I discovered I was pregnant that second time I knew
that I wanted to do things on my terms. I didn't know other
options or other ways to make life work out and I certainly
did not feel worthy of being a parent. But I knew that I
needed to do it my way with my decision-making. And so, I
didn't tell anyone. Not a single friend. Not a parent. No one.
Not siblings. I kept it completely to myself.

I immediately packed up my Chevy Chevette (a lemon from
the day I bought it used) with everything that could possibly
fit in there that I thought I would need. I had to start the car
by taking the screwdriver and connecting it between the
solenoid and the starter because the ignition switch would
not work.

I had six hundred dollars total to my name and I took off.

I find it interesting as I was researching, trying to go through
past journals, songs I wrote or any writings I have kept,
there is a lot. I was very surprised to discover I only had one
journal entry, nothing else. I'll admit my journal keeping

was a bit sporadic but during times of trial or great emotion, I wrote. Writing is my way of venting. The most interesting thing about this is I was so determined to keep this a secret that I wouldn't even allow myself to write about it in my private journal. This shows how fractured I became. It wasn't that these sides of myself were not true, I did have these thoughts, but it felt like they were happening to someone else.

I was a woman who was pregnant. Who had nobody. Again…

In April, after ending up in Dallas, Texas, I wrote the following journal entry just months before I was going to give birth.

"Long time. I'm in Dallas Texas. Briefly after moving to Spokane, I realized my life was not going to bring me happiness. I guess once again, the Lord is blessing me by chastising me. For certain reasons I decided to leave Spokane. I considered going to Dallas just for fun (because of the TV show), but look, here I am.

I drove here from Spokane. I spent four days in Seattle, two in Portland, and seventeen days in San Diego with my grandma and grandpa. Then I headed for Texas. Grandma K gave me money for motels. Well, the drive was good except in Sweetwater, Texas 200 miles from Dallas, my car completely died.

There I was stranded. I called (from a pay phone on the side of the rode) Grandma crying and she calmed me down. Finally, a policeman picked me up and took me to a motel. The next day my grandma arranged for a tow truck and had it fixed.

I really felt lonely.

I also learned a lesson. There were two ways to look at the situation: negative, all mad because I had car trouble with no one around and not too much money, or positive, that I wasn't stranded on the road. I could call Grandma. And the Lord sent people to help me out.

The positive made life much more bearable. I must use that in all I do.

I'm staying with a family. They are friends of my dad's from when they were first married. They have been so good to me. They make me feel so welcome.

There are some things I want to do when I'm married, like keep a family journal and write in it once a week for family home evening. And make church and conference talks fun by having a game session afterwards with $1 and $10 questions. Even though there's no real money, it's fun to answer the questions and better stresses the message."

The reality was that I fought like crazy to maintain that spiritual side of me. But it was going away. That was such a big part of me, and I was losing it. I got a job. I didn't tell them that I was having a baby. I didn't tell the people I was living with that I was pregnant. They had a daughter my age and we shared a room. I always dressed in the bathroom. I was always at work early.

Even while dressing frumpy, there came a point where I couldn't hide it anymore. People were starting to notice. I wasn't just overweight; I was pregnant, and I finally let people know. I explained that my intentions were to give the child up for adoption. I
planned on going through my Church's social services, as I did with the first child, and I contacted them. They set me up with healthcare in a public hospital.

That was not idyllic. It was a great learning experience for me. I got to see how medical care is for those who don't have insurance. For those who are poor and the difference between the care given to them and those who could pay more.

But the whole time, I never even allowed myself to think any other thought but that I was putting this child up for adoption. I was not capable of being a parent. Definitely not as a single parent.

Eventually, I was able to move out … and I got a roommate, someone that I met through work.

I remember the night that my water broke. I was home by myself. I don't know where my roommate was, perhaps she was working. I got up and I drove myself to the hospital, about an hour away. And I walked in. They saw my water had broken. The contractions hadn't really started too strongly so they just put me up in a room.

I thought I could do it by myself.

One thing that the social services did provide was, not necessarily a therapist, but a contact that I could work with. Someone who could drive me to appointments or talk to if necessary, and until that point I hadn't really taken advantage of that. But I decided that next morning, after a very long night, I didn't want to be alone and called her. She immediately came to the hospital, and I will forever be grateful to her for that as well as the times she would help me over the next year.

So, I didn't have to be completely alone. By that time they had started me on Pitocin, and I felt the contractions were coming pretty hard. I remember when she got there, they said it was going to be awhile until the delivery because the contractions were just starting. However, within the hour I was ready to deliver. Just as they started wheeling me down the hall, I suddenly had this overwhelming desire to hold that child in. I couldn't let go.

And until that moment it never even occurred to me…

And all the pain from the child before…

And the knowledge of the pain that I was going to have, overtook me.

I began to have this war with the doctor where I crossed my legs as he
tried to get me to open my legs and push. I remember them wheeling me down the hall because things were happening so fast. Way faster than they were ready for. And I was trying to keep myself covered with the sheet and they kept pulling the sheet up because they were afraid that I was going to deliver in the hall, and I kept pushing the sheet down. The minute they got me to the delivery room and moved from the
gurney to the table…

I delivered a baby boy.

The hospital staff knew that I had intentions of putting the child up for adoption. They asked me if I wanted to hold him. Though, I did… so much…I was too overwhelmed in that moment. I couldn't even speak. So, I shook my head, no, but I looked over where he lay, and here was this newborn, baby. I knew how newborn babies acted. I've had them since. I've been privileged enough to be with women when they've delivered. I also was the oldest of seven. With amazement this newborn boy lifted is head, turned and looked directly at me as if to say, "I'm yours".

I recall them moving me to a room that had so many people in there and we were just separated by curtains. We had all recently given birth. And then kindly, instead of keeping me in the same wing with all the other mothers, they put me with women that had other surgeries like hysterectomies. This allowed me to get away from babies crying, reminding me that I was about to go home without a newborn.

After I was able to rest a little, just dozing in and out. I was trying so hard not to deal with the emotions that were beginning to engulf me. Later that night - he was born in the afternoon - suddenly, a baby boy was being wheeled into my room by the nurse.
And she was going on and on about how she couldn't believe she'd gotten a phone call from me and how many times she had seen moms leave the hospital without holding their baby. It had always made her sad because she thought that they'd regret that,
and she was so grateful that I called and said that I wanted to hold my baby.

But I hadn't called. Still, I was so grateful he was there. I was so grateful for the opportunity. I held him, and I sang to him every lullaby I ever knew. And I prayed and prayed that someday he would be listening to the radio, and he would hear my voice and he would recognize it. He would know… that it was me… and he would feel love.

And I… I was very convinced he would be loved, and he would be raised by parents much more qualified than I was. So, I knew I was doing what was best for him. But I wanted him to know that I loved him. And I kept him as long as I was physically capable. He never cried. He just listened. And finally, as the nurse came to take him, I sobbed.

Towards the afternoon of the next day, (I'm sure it's no surprise that it
had been a very emotional night and morning) the next thing I knew the
baby boy was brought in, this time in a bassinet and a bathtub, all the
things to bathe and feed him. And then a different nurse said to me "We were all so delighted to get this call that you wanted to give this baby a bath. He's such a special baby." But again, I hadn't called.

So, we both prepared all the things necessary to give him a bath. "Do you know how to do this?" the nurse kindly asked. I assured her I did; I was the oldest of six, about to be seven, kids.

The irony was that during my whole process of being pregnant, my mother was also pregnant. She still didn't

know that I was with child and on our limited phone calls,
(fortunately, long distance calling was so expensive) I could
still pretend with her.
Whenever she would send letters complaining about her
pregnancy, I would secretly laugh because I was going
through the same thing. My little brother was born two
weeks after my delivery.

The nurse left me to it. And I was left to spend the day with
this sweet l little boy. I bathed him, dressed him, and I again
sang every song I could sing to him. I talked to him, and I
tried to listen. I fed him. Eventually, the woman arrived to
take me home and they took him away.

I left the hospital with such a broken heart.

I felt gratitude that I had that opportunity to spend that time
with him. I tried to feel gratitude that he was going to a
family that would love him as much as he deserved to be
loved. With a heart so… so broken, I remember that kind
woman took me home and wanted to stay with me, but I… I
sent her away, so I could be alone. All that evening
everything felt wrong. I could feel no comfort.

So, I called up my church leader and I asked if I could make
an appointment with him. Until that time, I don't think I had
ever met him. He agreed to see me immediately. At that
appointment, I told him the situation that I was in and what
had occurred at the hospital. I shared that I was really

struggling with my decision. In the kindest, most Christlike manner… He did not try to convince me. He listened. He showed love and compassion.

Then he said to me, "Deb I'm going to get up and I am going to walk into the chapel, and I am going to pray. And while I am there, I want you to stay in this office and I want you to pray. And I want you to ask your Heavenly Father what He wants you to do." Hearing the bishop explain that he not only loved and cared about me, but that God cared, knew and loved me, was in direct contrast to the image I had of God as a mean creator.

I was terrified. Because I knew Heavenly Father…at least I thought I did… He was mean.

I had to know what the right answer was. I reminded myself of what I had just heard. God loved me. So, after the bishop left, I carefully knelt down and began to pray.

Before I was even able to ask the question, an angel appeared to me. He told me the baby boy was to be my baby boy. That I was to be responsible for him. And we begin to carry on a conversation. A conversation in which I had questions… just being so incredulous. I couldn't believe it.

"What was I going to do with daycare?" I was promised I would be able to find day care for him all the time that I needed it. It was a promise that was kept.

"How can I do this? I barely even make enough money to get by myself." I was promised that means would be provided. It was a promise that was kept.

But most of all I was assured, that he was sent to me. That I was going to be the mother he needed. That I had all the gifts and talent to be his mother. And that his name was to be Ronald Christopher. Chris was the first of my major miracles.

It was not easy. I did have daycare. He was never abused. He was provided for.
Conditions were not always the best. In the beginning, we lived in an apartment. I once woke up in the night to feed him only to find roaches (my biggest nightmare, bugs that crunch) crawling over him. After that, I had him sleep with me in my bed with a can of Raid until we were able to move, probably a year or so later, to a better apartment.

More recently, as I have been shown the vision again and have been able to retain more and understand better, I was shown…"Chris, your child, in the premortal earth life was given special instructions. You needed him to help you become the woman you were meant to be. You will find your way back to Me because you loved him more than yourself."

I wish I could say after the time I was visited by that angel in the bishop's office, that I saw God as a loving God. But I still wasn't capable… life was too hard.

But I was grateful. I knew God loved me, and was definitely aware of me, but I still saw
Him as mean.

However, it was also during the time with Chris, being a single parent, that I developed such a close relationship with my Savior Jesus Christ. I made Him the patriarch of my home. I could only go for decisions, outside of my own mind, to Him in prayer and scripture. That's how I developed that very close relationship.

The angel was right on all things. I did go to church. Because I needed to take my son to church. I could stay within true principles that I knew were true because I knew that was what I wanted to have for him. I did a lot of backsliding over the first few years, maybe at the time I didn't feel worthy of anything. But Chris definitely was.

And because he was, I had to continue to act as if I was and each time, I would begin to lose faith, I was brought back to be the mom he deserved.

I worked for a very difficult company at the time who wanted to fire me after I chose to keep Chris but that wasn't legal. They did what they could to make things difficult for me. Putting me on night shift and then changing the schedule without even a 24 hour notice. They were men with a great deal of money who wouldn't pay their employees. But despite that, they eventually did something wonderful for me. They moved me to a place I never thought I'd go, but exactly where I was meant to be…Las Vegas.

> *"Maybe you'll get a replacement,*
> *there's plenty like me to be found*
> *Monorails who aint got a penny*
> *sniffing for tit-bits like you on the ground"*
> -Goodbye Yellow Brick-

Chapter Twenty-One
Getting Out of Dodge

"He over-cometh all, He saveth from the Fall
His Might and Power are Great
He all things did create."
-A Mighty Fortress Is Our God-

I knew I needed to get out of Dallas. Most of the men that I dated were abusive. It sounds so horrible to say now, but I felt most comfortable with that type of man, because I knew how to do that kind of relationship. Even though I knew that wasn't how I wanted a connection to be, or raise my son in, it was still where my social comfort level kept me. I really knew nothing of a healthy relationship between a male and female.

I had male friends. However, as soon as I or he would try to take it to a level of boyfriend and girlfriend things went downhill fast. Looking back the pattern was usually the same. The guy would start to get controlling (disguised as caring so much he wanted to spend every moment with me.) This usually meant I had no time for my own friends (isolation). Next came the push to have more of a physical relationship than I wanted. Inevitably, the violence began. I knew there were good men out there. I had my friend Wayne prove that; I believe I just didn't feel worthy of them.

In Dallas, I did have really good friends that cared about me. However, the ones that had similar belief systems and values were married. As I reflect on those friends though, they did some incredible things for me. A great example of this happened when one guy, who I had ended things with, pushed his way into my apartment and beat me up. I went into past trauma mode. My sister and her husband (fiancé at the time) called the cops and came over to watch Chris while I went to a job interview. (I didn't get it. The bruises may have turned them off, though I had used the original excuse of falling down the stairs.)

Another married couple came over and took Chris and I to a hotel for the night. The next day when I got back to my apartment my friends had moved all my stuff out so I could not be located. That was such a wonderful thing and such a wonderful blessing.

Despite those friends, I was so relieved when the company that I worked for transferred me to Las Vegas. What they didn't know, what only a couple knew, was that I was pregnant…Again…

"Turn me loose, from your hand
Let me fly to distant lands…
Fly away, skyline pigeon fly
Towards the dreams You've left so very far behind"
-Skyline Pigeon Fly-

Chapter Twenty-Two
Home at Last

"So, I'll cherish the old rugged cross
Till my trophies at last I lay down
I will cling to the old rugged cross
And exchange it someday for a crown."
-The Old Rugged Cross-

Though I would arrive in Vegas under some quite difficult circumstances, my healing began the moment I arrived. As Chris and I drove to the hotel, I knew I'd found my home. It was the first place I'd ever been with an environment where I did not feel judged. Everywhere I went I would see such opposition.

The first step I took when I got my apartment was to locate my church. That gave me a firm social base. However, this is where things get a little bit sticky. I completely denied to myself that I was pregnant. Even for me it is hard to understand how I could split my brain up so concretely. It was some extreme form of compartmentalization. I would not allow myself to recognize the changes in my body or think about what was to come during most of the first 7 months. I didn't even see a doctor.

(OK. Stepping out of the story again for a minute. You must be saying to yourself, "What the heck Deb. Have you ever heard of birth control?" Honestly, I really didn't know a lot. The only thing I had ever been taught was abstinence. I knew there was Planned Parenthood, but at the time I couldn't go there because abortion was out of the question, so thought I couldn't go there for anything.

But the biggest reason was, I was never going to do it again. I knew premarital sex was wrong. I didn't even like it. I even tried to stop it. Also, keep in mind that stuff like this was not on TV yet. There was no internet available to me. It really was different then. Things are so very different now. Yes, it is crazy to think that a female who was so smart, graduated in the top of her class, did well in college, held very responsible jobs and treasured her spirituality, couldn't stop herself from getting pregnant. I guess I'm glad that currently, as I'm perusing my journals, even I can't put myself back in her place.

I can spout out the psychology of it. Oh, but trust me, I get the insanity of it. Ok back to the story.)

Of course, I knew I would have to explain why suddenly I was changing jobs… and shapes. I didn't think people would think it was a tumor. The truth is I knew from the very beginning that this was not going to be my baby. Every time I would pray, I would get that answer often in ways that were undeniable. However, I was unclear about the rest of things.

There was a married couple I knew well. And I planned with every intention to be their surrogate. She could no longer have kids. She had one child from her first marriage and had just married about a year before. She was a good friend; they were very kind. I had worked with her husband and knew he was a good man. (This actually was the couple who had took Chris and me to the hotel after the attack in Dallas.)

As the delivery got a bit closer, I started to worry a little. Maybe a better way to put it is that I just felt completely unsettled each time we communicated. Things just started to feel very wrong. There was absolutely nothing flawed with them. They were a wonderful couple. I couldn't understand why I was feeling like I was about to make an egregious mistake. Now, I can recognize how much my Father in Heaven was watching over me. He knew how it would have been very difficult for me to know who had a child of mine. Even though I could separate the baby from being a child that I just carried, it was going to be too much for me to know the people who were blessed to raise that child.

So, I had to tell those dear friends that I wouldn't be able to do that. I am sure it broke their hearts and I'm deeply sorry. I lost contact with them after that. I have held on to the faith that the Lord would bless them for their kindness. I know I did what was right but I am sad that I had hurt them. Since that time, I've had the privilege of working with foster care and children in group homes. There are a lot of children that need good families. I have no doubt that couple have offered their home to many.

I felt inspired to contact the church social services again. I didn't tell anyone I was doing anything different, so the surrogate story just stayed out there. It really wasn't anyone else's business. This decision was between me and God. As the time approached to deliver the baby, the only person that I had confided in was Kalene, my friend from college. She came up and stayed with me just after I had the baby.

It was (actually it still is) hard to know that I was doing what God wanted, but not being given a way to avoid the pain for myself and others. I've heard many people tell me that I deserved to suffer because I was sexually promiscuous. I've actually been told I haven't suffered enough. I think those people are just very cruel.

I knew that my baby girl was not meant to grow up with me. I also was keenly aware of how much I would suffer because of that. I couldn't help but hope that maybe God would change His mind. I also had my experience with Chris to look back on. Thus, as soon as I was released from the hospital, Kalene, Chris and I went to a beautiful majestic place called "Red Rocks" just on the outskirts of Las Vegas, so that I would be sure of my decision.

We parked under some of the rocks and there was a place where I could very easily climb up, because I just had a baby. Kalene stayed down to play with Chris. I would go up and pray, then I would come down to play with Chris and talk with Kalene. Then I'd go back up and then come back down. It seemed like we spent the whole day doing that. The answer did not come as it did with Chris. But it did come and there was no doubt. I was to put the baby up for adoption.

I wrote her a letter and kept a copy for myself. I hope her mom gave it to her. I'd like to think she got a little bit advice from me. I'd like to think she knew that I cared so much about her the whole time.

Yes, I am crying as I write this. There is so much pain in losing a child no matter the circumstances. Still, I know I did what God told me to do. And the grief I feel when I think of this baby girl is different. I received direct revelation telling me to put my baby up for adoption. I never got that witness for the first little girl I had. Maybe my mom and dad did. I wouldn't know because I was never allowed to talk about it. Because I had no choice in the matter, I was stuck in the "anger" stage of grief. I'm able to pull myself out quickly now. But it took years to reach that stage.

I've had the great blessing of attending many adoption hearings since then. I've seen their joy, and I hold onto that. I still say a special prayer for them on their birthdays.

Sometimes I still cry over them. Though I know I did the right thing, I have not been spared the grief. The anger of that grief could only be directed towards myself and God as I saw things then. We were the only ones involved in the decision. Truth was, I began to hate us both.

(Stepping back out of the story, I'm sure you are wondering why I haven't tried to find them now that it is so easy with DNA. The biggest reason is because I know they went to the parents they were supposed to have. I know that those girls were sealed to the parents that they were supposed to be sealed to, and I know that means that they are with that family for time and all eternity.

However, I would be lying if I didn't admit there was another reason. I'm afraid. What if I find that either of them has suffered from feeling unloved because they were adopted? Then everything that I believed and held on to get me through this would be a lie. If I found they were abused, how would I live with myself? If, and this is the most realistic of my fears, they don't feel unloved, they don't really need that connection because they already have a family, they have had good lives with children of their own, then wouldn't it be more loving for me to allow them their peace and not try to insert myself? I've unsealed my part of the adoption records so they could contact me if they needed to. I'm a little bit afraid of the pain either way.

But I don't know. My own kids are older now. Perhaps future generations will contact each other. Who knows? That may be another part of my story.)

"While Mona Lisas and Mad Hatters Sons of Bankers Sons of Lawyers
Turn around and say good morning to the light
For unless they see the sky, but they can't and that is why
They know not if it's dark outside or light."
-Mona Lisas and Mad Hatters-

Chapter Twenty-Three
Viva Las Vegas

"Come thou fount of every blessing
Tune my heart to sing Thy Grace
Streams of mercy, never ceasing
Call for songs of Loudest Praise"
-Come Thou Font of Every Blessing-

I got a job at an actuarial firm, training to be an actuary for retirement plans of all things. Hurray to being good at math. Boo to not being good enough. I never became an actuary.

However, I was able to buy my own condominium. I will never forget how good it felt to sit in the middle of the empty living room knowing that I owned it. I had done it all by myself. It felt so marvelous. I was beginning to feel good about myself.

As I mentioned when I first arrived in Vegas, the "opposition in all things" was wonderful. I was able to go to church on Sunday and have an incredible spiritual experience. Yet then on the drive home from church I would look over at the bus next to me, and there'd be these extremely scantily clad women on the side. It let me know that I could hold onto the good, special and sacred to me in a place where distractions abound. I appreciated the overtness of it all. It felt so genuine to me. I didn't have any judgment for them, nor did I feel judgment from them. Perhaps, it was a place where "good" and "evil" had developed a way to co-exist.

The environment was a direct reflection of the turmoil I was feeling inside. Las Vegas gave me hope. If all these people could figure out how to reconcile the differences, maybe I could find a way to reconcile myself.

> *"I have to say my friends, we're looking for a light ahead*
> *In the distance a candle burns,*
> *Salvation keeps the hungry children fed."*
> -Salvation-

Chapter Twenty-Four
Carma My Karma

"I stand all amazed at the love Jesus offers me
Confused at the grace that so fully He proffers me."
-I Stand All Amazed-

I met Carma.

I realize there will not be a way for me to convey to you how much those three words mean. She was and remains my gift from God. Carma was assigned to be my "visiting teacher," now referred in my religion as a "ministering sister." That meant she was assigned by one of our church leaders to come and visit me once a month and if I had a need the church could help with, she would help facilitate that.

Looking at it with logic, I can see why the leaders would have assigned her to me. We were both single parents and not even two months apart in age. Oh, but I know better. She was divinely appointed. We had promised each other as spirits before we came to earth, that we would be there for one another. The two of us learned to navigate our way into being the kind of women that we wanted to be.

There are so many words yet, even if I wrote every one of them, I could not do justice to how blessed my life became with her friendship. I will just say,

Thank you, Carma. I love you.

"And I would have walked head on
To the deep end of the river."
-Someone Saved My Life Tonight-

Chapter Twenty-Five
Help, I Need a Doctor

"Jesus, take the wheel, take it from my hands
'Cause I can't do this on my own"
-Jesus Take the Wheel-

During the final part of that pregnancy, Chris started having some ear problems. Both of us were fish, we were in the pool all the time. So, I just thought maybe his ears weren't draining and was advised to use alcohol drops in his ears after he swam. We did that faithfully, but his ears kept draining quite a bit and eventually there became a pretty bad smell. He was almost three years old when this started.

I had to try to figure out what was wrong with his ears. So, I took him to a local doctor, and they said he obviously would need tubes put in. My sister happened to work in California for a well-known audiologist. She made arrangements with him, and I went to San Diego to get tubes put in his ears with confidence.

The doctor came out of the surgery and said he couldn't finish the procedure. Chris had a condition called "Congenital" meaning it happened within the womb, "Bilateral," meaning that it was on both sides, "Cholesteatoma," which is a tumor. That form of tumor itself is not cancerous. But because of the way it gathers and grows, it eats everything around it. It would eventually eat all the ear bones, all the meatus, which is that styrofoamy stuff surrounding the bones and penetrate into this brain. The tumors, of course, would have to be removed.

The first two surgeries were done In San Diego. The man was not a compassionate surgeon by any means. I was more concerned with his skill. My sister worked for him, so I thought Chris might get some extra attention and care. But he was everything that makes our American medical world as awful as it is. He was an arrogant surgeon. Who thought he was God.

After Chris' second surgery, the doctor had done something that was completely against what we had agreed on and I knew it was very unnecessary. When I complained to him, he asked me where I got the audacity to say something to him. He actually said that word. I ended up screaming down the hospital hall – "Audacity, have you forgotten you work for me? I pay your bill. You're my son's doctor. I employ you." I was only 25 trying to navigate a very frightening medical world. However, I was also a mom who knew how to fight. That was me being passionate in a place where I probably could have held back. But I did get an ovation from the hospital staff, so I don't think he was very well liked.

However, that meant he could no longer be Chris' doctor and that was a cause for panic. That doctor had assured me he was the best. If the "best" couldn't be trusted, then what was I to do? (He lied.) As promised by that angel the means were provided.

I came back to work, and I shared with my employers what had gone on. The owner of the company happened to know, play golf with and did the pension plan for the head of the "House Ear Clinic". A clinic that is a world renowned for its work with ears.

Chris got the best medical care that you could get in the world. Literal royalty was flown in for ear surgeries with his doctor. Or if they were real big wigs, like the ones in Saudi Arabia, his doctor was flown there.

So, between the ages of three and eight Chris had 15 surgeries. I traveled to Los Angeles for every surgery. While I was able to have my grandma there in San Diego, I would be alone with Chris for the rest of his surgeries. In LA, my parents never came, even though my mom and dad lived less than an hour away from the hospital.

That hurt.

While we waited for him to go into surgery, I'd make up games. One of them was "thumb or finger." I pulled my eyelashes out and I would press them to my finger and thumb, then Chris would guess if it would stick to my thumb or finger. I can't tell you how many times I would look in the mirror and notice gaps in my lashes from playing that game.

I'd sit there by myself and wait for him to come out of surgery. That desolate experience was a hard thing to do by myself. With each surgery, the news became progressively more difficult. It seemed like every time they would come out and tell me "Okay madam, this time the tumor has wrapped itself around the facial nerve. And the doctor's doing everything he can to separate it without causing damage to the facial nerve, but it was too enmeshed, so I am afraid half of his face is going to be paralyzed."

They were so sure.

I would accept it, but not before sitting there and trying to memorize every movement and twitch his face would make when he was happy. Or the way his eyebrows would raise when he would cry. Or the way his eyes would squint so tight when he would sneeze. I would sit there and wait, replaying those facial movements in my head until he would come out of surgery. Miraculously, each time that he did, I would say "Please smile for Mom" and he would.

The last four surgeries were especially difficult. Not only had they convinced me that Chris' face would be paralyzed, but that it was becoming noticeably harder to wake Chris from his anesthesia. With each surgery they were needing to keep him under longer as the procedures became increasingly more difficult and time consuming. The tumors were getting more intricate and harder to remove without doing major damage.

Then the nurse would call me to come back because they had really struggled to wake him up and they thought maybe I could get him to come out of it. So, utterly terrified, I would go back and with all the bravery I could muster I would say to him, "Chris, can you please wake up? And can you smile for Mom? You don't have to talk. I just need you to show me how you smile. Mom's been a little sad and she needs to see you smile."

I kept repeating that. Urging a little bit stronger each time. Until finally he would wake up. Sometimes it took a scary amount of time. I remember one time in particular he really wasn't coming out of the anesthesia and his vitals were dropping. I could tell the nurse was getting a little panicky. Chris' head was covered in these big, huge bandages. All I could see was just his little round face. I tried to hold his hand but that was covered because it was taped to a board under his arm to keep his IV steady. The only place I could get to was his feet. I remember rubbing his feet and just saying, "Chris it's time to wake up and mommy needs to see you smile."

He didn't wake up. After several attempts, I had to get a little bit mad, and using a harsher tone (plus I was beginning to panic), I said, "Chris it's time for you to come back. You need to talk to your mom. Your mom is telling you to come here." He opened his eyes and he smiled and said, "Mom, I'm having a conversation with Jesus and you're interrupting."

He did receive a miracle that day as he had on so many occasions. I too received a miracle that day.

After seeing that Chris was able to wake up and smile, the nurse suggested I go get something to drink while she got him set up in his room. By this time, we had gotten to know the nursing staff. She could probably tell I was about to fall to the ground in a blubbering mess. I unconsciously agreed and started walking down the halls. I had no idea where I was going, I'm not even sure I was aware I was walking. I couldn't even cry. I was so very tired, so…so… afraid and felt so… so… so… alone.

Something whispered for me to look up. At the end of what seemed a mile long hallway, was a figure. I knew I needed to get to that person. When I reached her, I fell into her arms and sobbed. I don't know how long she held me like that. It was as long as I needed. I began to realize I had not greeted this person… and wait did I even
know who this was? It was Kalene's mom. She was my angel that day. I recognized her spirit before I was able to see her physically.

(Stepping out of story, I learned so much from watching Kalene and being a part of their family. It was the first time I had witnessed a functional family. Thank you, Kalene, for sharing your family. Thank you for telling your mom. Thank you, Kalene's Mom for being my mom that day. I love you all.)

Though Chris has no natural method at all to amplify sound he was able to hear. The doctors throughout the rest of his childhood were incredulous. They couldn't explain it.
I understood completely.

He was a miracle.

> *"Took the grand prize you and your eyes, butterfly light*
> *Escaping the reach of their fangs and their claws*
> *Such a pale little thing in your lily-white skin*
> *High up on the diving board."*
> -The Diving Board-

Chapter Twenty-Six
Can We Talk?

"He clothes the lilies of the field, He feeds the birds in the sky
And He will feed those who trust Him,
And guide them with His eye."
-Consider the Lilies-

Eventually though, the amount of time spent traveling back and forth for surgeries, appointments and recovery time, took too great a toll on my job. I was let go. I began working from home selling skin care. This was a blessing in many ways, though I didn't know that the day I lost my job.

God was giving me the actual time, not just the opportunity, to begin to heal. I now had some time during the day where I could focus more intentionally on putting myself together. The extra time was spent on all things therapy.

Therapy had been suggested to me when working with the church social services in Las Vegas. They strongly encouraged it. I didn't have the time before nor did I trust therapy after what it did to me in college. I called them and set up an appointment. I met with my therapist once a week. During the rest of the week, I would do "homework," sometimes it was letters, other times getting myself a treat. One time it was to list 100 things I did right. That was enlightening. I was able to work through so many things.

Most of all I was able to get an understanding of why I was repeating
behaviors.

I learned the difference between transgressions and reactions. I was so blessed to get a good therapist. (They aren't easy to find but they are out there.) If you have been the victim of incest, sexual abuse or any kind of abuse, it's important to find a therapist. Do not count on a clergyman because, unless your clergyman is a trained abuse therapist, they will not be able to help you in all the ways required. There will be more to address than just the spiritual part. God was definitely there, right next to me leading me. However, the emotional, mental and physical sides needed to be addressed. There were many things that I needed to do to heal, a great deal of that was part of this world, not just spiritual things.

I had to work very hard at it. I was a hard worker. I was beginning to understand myself, which began the journey to not only love myself, but also to begin earnestly to understand God. I really wanted to understand why so many were calling Him their
"Loving Heavenly Father."

My life was hard. I did have miracles, but I paid a high price for them. My dad used to quote to me a scripture all the time, "Where much is given, much is required." That was definitely true for me. I guess I wondered why His lessons

(if indeed that is what they were) had to be so harsh. I didn't see many others having the intensity of trials that I had to endure. Though I continued to think God was mean, I did begin to try to
understand why. That would turn out to be a very long journey. I was in for the long haul.

As I previously mentioned, one of the exercises I had to do was write letters. Some were to express gratitude to friends or people who had helped along the way. Those letters were easy, kind of fun even.

I also had to write letters to my abusers. Most of those weren't sent. However, there were some abusers that I had an ongoing relationship with, such as my parents. I was encouraged, when I felt ready, to read those letters out loud to the person responsible. It took me a couple years to be ready. I'm including parts of the letter I wrote to my mother. I've decided to do this because it will show just how angry and hurt I was at that time in my life. Anger was part of healing. It was a feeling I fought to suppress.
I did not want to be like my dad whose default emotion was anger. Yet, I was filled with rage. And that had to be released, hopefully in a healthy way, before it came out in a very dangerous way.

March 23

"Dear Mother,

It's been very hard for me to get in touch with my emotions enough for me to write this letter. However, I just finished reading the letter you wrote me … and I cannot stay quiet any longer.

In your letter you spoke of your pain, your anger, your tears and your difficulty to forgive.

You spoke of the sadness you felt losing a granddaughter.

It is beyond me how you could talk of loving me with all your heart and then be so selfish.

I want to tell you of my overwhelming anger, of my tremendous pain and torment, of my endless tears and suffering and most of all my reasons for being unable to forgive.

I pray that what I've learned is true. That by giving all of this back to you, I may be rid of it and be at peace with myself.

My anger and pain go back a long way.

As you are aware, I have been receiving counseling. It has given me the opportunity to discover a great deal about myself.

I have been able to sort out the difference between sins and responses. This realization has allowed me to repent for what I have done wrong, something I have tried to do in the past, yet I

was never able to feel clean because I kept trying to repent and not feel guilty for things that
weren't mine to repent from.

So much of my life has been a bad response to the destructive acts towards me. …

…I couldn't tell you I was afraid.

I guess even then at such an early age I knew you couldn't protect me.

How could I have believed any differently?

I knew you were a victim of your own. You couldn't protect yourself against Dad's abuse. I had seen him strangle you, hit you and verbally abuse you.

As you are aware, I had also felt Dad's rath. How could I have felt safe?

Now I have to say something here. I realize you were also a victim. I also have talked with Grandma, and she has given me some insight on how you were brought up and why that upbringing may have caused you to stay.

But you must also realize what allowing yourself to be a victim did to your children.

When I was young you lost my sense of feeling secure.

When I was older you lost my respect.

I am angry with you for that.

I am of course angry with my father too. But that pain goes much deeper, and I will deal with him on that.

And now the painful part begins.

… I'm sure most of the Dad's clan was affected by sexual abuse. I am also sure that Dad and his brothers and sisters were both victims and abusers. I know how hard it's been on my Aunt.

Yet because it was kept so secret as was the violence and verbal abuse, it was just passed on generation to generation.

But I promise you it will stop with my generation. No more secrets and no more lies.

When I was a little older the long-drawn-out sexual abuse with Uncle Keith began. How is it you could not see it or stop it?

I remember he would stay at our house. You would allow an innocent girl who didn't realize it, to wear a see-through green night gown in front of a boy who was very sexually active.

Perhaps you were naive. Such words like incest or sexual abuse never crossed your mind. But I find that hard to accept.

I look at Dad's family and so many signs are there.

I am so angry when I think of all the horribly accusing talk and rumors that went around about me and several of my cousins.

How stupid can you parents be?

Do you think that kids are just born evil?

Could you not see some horrible, wicked pattern in all of us?

Did you not for one minute wonder why, with all the gospel knowledge we were given, so many of us drank, got pregnant and have not been able to sustain intimate relationships?

What is the matter with you?

Did you not think that perhaps there was something wrong with what I was taught?

…Can you not see that though my consequences were more obvious, my brother and sisters are having the same problems, suffering the same pain, reacting with the same bad choices?

I see you close your eyes to all this.

When I was twelve, just as I was developing my own identity, I was also abused by another close member of the family. I will leave it up to him to tell you or not.

But I can tell you that at that point all my self-worth was shattered. I was taught that sex was bad, dirty, but the only way to get affection.

I desperately needed affection because I felt so ashamed and dirty for someone else's sin.

I can't even begin to comprehend why the mother of a Beehive president, in the Mia-maid presidency and having such a strong spirit, did not even question why her precious little girl went astray.

Instead, you judged me and made me out to be so bad, which only led me to be worse.

I began drinking as soon as I learned how easy it made the pain go away.

I drank a lot. I kept it in my closet. It made me feel good.

You never even noticed your daughter was on her way to becoming an alcoholic.

Then when I was seventeen, I went drinking with the wrong crowd. After a movie we went back to someone's apartment.

I didn't know where, nor did I care.

I was with the captain of the …football team and star quarterback. One of their dates passed out in the living room so they both came to me.

While one held my arms the other one raped me and so I lost my virginity…

…I didn't know about date rape. I screamed, cried and hurt.

I felt it was my fault for being in the wrong situation and I still believe that you and Dad would feel the same way.

It hurt to walk and sit down for a couple days, but you never noticed…

…You and Dad have always downplayed the violence in our home. But whether or not you admit it, I was physically, emotionally and sexually abused.

The law says it; the Church says it; and I say it.

You denied my fears of Dad. You even let him in the house one night so he could hit me. Perhaps you were more afraid of what he'd do to you.

But you were my mother. You should have protected me.

Perhaps now you have a glimpse of why I became sexually active, but you never questioned it then. If you did, you found all the cause was with me.

When I became pregnant you sent me away. It was a dirty little secret no one knew.

You lied to people about where I was and why I was there.

I think it's a bit ironic that you expressed such anger towards me for doing the same thing. You saw the pregnancy as the sin. After all that's what caused you the pain.

You never saw the pain I felt from incest, violence and lies.

You made me feel so ashamed and as if I was the only one who had ever brought disgrace to the family.

Imagine my surprise when I realized several months after Christopher was born that you had caused your family the same pain.

But it's OK for you to lie.

You also mentioned in your letter how I said I was sorry; I had talked to the bishop and repented and that was that.

You said that that wasn't enough for you; that you wanted to see me suffer, see more tears.

It is because of this that I can hardly call you mother. The word must be forced out of my mouth each time I say it.

How could you be so blind and hard hearted to my pain and suffering.

How could you have just overlooked the severe punishments I put myself through?

Do you even remember the day those two girls were born? Do you cry on those days every year? Do you weep each holiday for their loss? Do you lie awake every night after seeing a girl in the mall who is the same age and wonder about her and cry over her?

Are you there now even when I am married and doing everything the right way not getting pregnant until 4 months after we were married, and yet I feel nothing but shame and guilt instead of joy over the baby I am carrying now?

What kind of mother could wish her child could suffer more than I have and do now?

And I must wonder how you could deny the pain and anguish you have caused me and the rest of your children by raising us in a less than nurturing environment?

You should have stopped not only the physical but verbal abuse as well. You were the mother, and we were your responsibility.
I am the product of a dysfunctional home. I suffer for that now as I try to establish a relationship with my wonderful husband.

Corey suffers a great deal because of my lack of knowledge of what a good marital relationship is…

…Please, please stop being so selfish with your pain and problems and help the rest your kids to not have to suffer. God gave you stewardship over them. He expects you to love them and raise them correctly, in a safe environment. Nurture them, teach them how precious they are and at all times be aware of why they do what they do.

I must also add that your letter mentioned concern over Christopher and how he would feel towards me when he was older. How touching. I wonder if you hope that he will give me some of the pain you feel I've given you.

I am not worried.

I have been very open and honest about the other pregnancy and as his ability to comprehend grows, I teach him more and more.

It is because of my love for Christopher and my unyielding desire to raise him in a Christlike environment, that I feel such pain over what happened to me.

I have made sacrifices and some very terrifying choices because I wanted to do the best for him.

I expect nothing from you that I wouldn't do for my own children…

…So now I give back to you the judgement, the guilt, the anger and the pain.

They are yours to do with what you may. I have carried all this for too long.

I hope you find peace…

Sincerely,"

I do realize the letter is harsh. However, as I read through it, I wouldn't take any of it back. I am a mother and I know how a mother feels. (At least I know how I feel, and others have demonstrated the same love for their children.)

There was only one time when another Uncle, not mentioned before, tried to play with my breasts when I was about 16. I came home and told my mom. To her credit she did say something to someone. I don't know if it was my dad or the uncle. However, my dad's mom told her to be quiet, I was lying and that was the end of that.

I get that my mom was scared. Maybe she even felt trapped at times. A mother should protect her children. No one will ever convince me otherwise.

"Cold, cold heart, hard done by you
Some things look better baby, just passing through…
But it's no sacrifice, no sacrifice, It's no sacrifice at all."
-Sacrifice-

Chapter Twenty-Seven
14 Generations

*"You're a good, good Father, it's who you are, it's who you are
And I'm loved by you, it's who I am, it's who I am."*
-Good, Good Father-

The Scriptures give us two principles that might appear contradictory. The first is that man will be punished for his own sins and not for Adams transgression. The second is the sins of the fathers shall be visited upon the children. The resolution of this contradiction is in recognizing consequences.

We will not be held accountable, or judged by God for the sins of the generations before us. However, we can definitely suffer from the consequences of prior generations. The best most obvious example of this is the decision made by Eve and then Adam to partake of the forbidden fruit. Because of their choice, a courageous loving self-sacrificing choice, all mankind was changed. Our spirits were able to come down to earth to a body that was mortally flawed. We then were allowed to do what we chose to do, because of the free agency given to us.

Our bodies are not perfect. We were gifted with our imperfect body; the imperfections cause us to overcome weaknesses, forcing us to grow. They push us to find understanding, thus we gain knowledge. And in that way become more like God.

We accept that their choice had tremendous effects on all future generations of the earth. The option they chose was to literally change their physical bodies into ones of imperfection, and capable of death, consequently, changing the rest of the people that would come to earth.

I have so much gratitude for Eve's ability and willingness to put their comfort aside to achieve the greater commandment of multiplying and replenishing the earth. This required them to have to completely change physically to a flawed mortal body. What a sacrifice.

We all have been burdened by flaws; some are just inherent to mortality; others are because they are passed onto us from our mortal parents.

God, of course was aware of that. He made sure we could overcome both the physical and spiritual shortcomings, with the Atonement of Jesus Christ. In the vision I had, a lot of time was spent on this concept. (In fact, as I mentioned in the introduction, I originally thought this was what I was to write the book about, like a research paper.)

The Lord showed me generations to numerous for me to count. Each generation had been genetically programmed with glitches from the sins of generations before. Personality traits were passed, some like triumphant torches; other traits appeared as a flawed link in a chain used to trip or hold back future generations.

We were born with specific good traits and bad traits; a proclivity to addictions of all manner, some diseases, and even the weakness that if not checked, leads to abuse. Still the link of abuse running in the DNA of prior generations, kept secret for so long became invisible or unable to be seen for what it was. Seldom, if ever was abuse looked at head-on. In fact, quite the opposite. The abuse, after so many generations of occurrence became normalized.

This led the following generation to not only have to deal with the abuse perpetrated on them, but they also had to fight their own inclinations to abuse. And no one was given the tools to deal with either.

Here's another way to look at it. My husband's mother had type two diabetes. She had been diagnosed with it at a fairly young age. There was a defective gene that had been passed to her that caused her to not produce the correct amount of insulin. That gene was passed to my husband and probably onto his kids. Corey's body has the inclination to suffer the same way his mother did, eventually dying from complications caused the disease. However, unlike his mother, as soon as Corey saw lab results showing he was heading down that same road, he drastically changed his diet and exercise. Thus, though he still has the faulty gene, he will not have to endure the consequences of that disease. Better still, Corey is teaching what he learns to our children. That way no future generation will have to suffer from that particular condition.

With Corey's mother, modern medicine gave her the diagnosis, but she chose to ignore it; often tried to defy it. However, that did not make it go away. What would have happened if Corey chose to ignore it? Well, yes, he probably would have lost his eyesight, maybe some limbs, and would feel ill every day for the rest of his life. Now take this example further, what would happen to future generations? They might just think things are what they are; I'm going to get sick - the older I get the worse life is going to be, because my body just won't work. The notion seems ludicrous.

The inclination to abuse is much like the gene for diabetes. It had been passed down for so long that in my dad's family it just was the way it was. But it wasn't! Or at least it did not have to be that way. Admitting the propensity for abuse is like admitting there are gigantic ugly monsters under the bed we sleep in. It is far easier to ignore, defend or rationalize the behaviors.

I was shown 14 generations had the penchant for abuse. I want to be very clear, in my vision, at no time were any acts

of abuse justified or excused; actually, I learned quite the opposite. We are all expected to overcome the mortal man. I see abuse as a very
obvious addiction to overcome. This is another excerpt from my journal after I had the vision.

"In my vision, the specific generations I remember were the ones from my Great Grandmother (on my dad's side on down to my generation. She was the 4th generation from me. It was clearly explained that she had been born with the same genetic defect…
…The understanding was given to me in a similar way as the prior. Yet, it seemed to be much easier and faster. I'm sure it was because I didn't have to keep going back over and over. I was shown, understood and moved on…to be shown the abuse that occurred to them causing their behavior.

Again, at no time did I feel that an excuse was made. I just understood that when it did come time to pass judgement on the prior generations all of this would be considered.

However, viewing their abuse did give me the compassion I needed to let go of the hate and judgement I had for them. It was also pointed out that each generation did try to improve on the generation before it. I was shown several examples of my dad protecting some of his siblings. Still, when faced with the temptation himself he was
weak and did not live up to the promises he made in heaven.

It was then explained to me that I had accepted the mission to stop the generational abuse. I was to bring it to light, and not repeat it. I made that promise as did many of my cousins. We accomplished what we said we would do." Since then, I have heard of abusive situations still taking place. However, I recognize how differently things are handled both for the victim and the abuser. There are no longer secrets about any of it. The abuser is held accountable and most of all the victim is validated and if necessary (the usual case) therapy is immediately required.

God did not intend for the family to be lost. He began to place specific warrior spirits that could overcome those imperfect defective bodies. I was shown in my vision how strong the spirits of my father's generation were, they were unable to overcome and conquer all physical baggage. However, they did recognize it and had the capacity to raise the next generation of greater and stronger spirits who would be given the ability to stop…And stare the gruesome beast in the face. That generation was my generation.

But I couldn't begin to know all of this as I began my healing journey. All I knew then was that it was time for me to take the first step, even if it was into the dark where I may not be able to see where I was going for a while. I just needed to begin.

Las Vegas was that place for me, and a part of me will be there forever.

I was very nervous about driving there with all my belongings that first time. The whole way there I kept thinking "is this right?" But as I look back on it, I can't think of a kinder, better thing the Lord could have done for me than to move me to Las Vegas.

It's where I had my first experience with the temple. It's where I met my husband. A lot of good things happened for me in Las Vegas, and I will be forever grateful

"I go to search for the yellow moon and the fathers of our sons
Where the red sun sinks in the hills of gold and the healing waters run."
-Indian Sunset-

Chapter Twenty-Eight
How I Met Corey

"All creatures of our God and King
Lift up your voice and with us sing
Alleluia! Alleluia!
-All Creatures of our God and King-

If I were to write a love story that had all the suspense, drama, comedy, heartache, mystery, thrills and passion, I would write about my own marriage. Ours is quite a love story.

I used to sell skincare by going into people's homes and putting on a demonstration. As part of my routine, I would joke quite a bit about being single and getting ready for a date, allowing me to bring in why a particular product was so important. It was a good way to get the group to feel comfortable and that led to better sales. The downside was that a lot of people wanted to set me up with someone.

There was one specific demonstration I did that had record sales. I didn't know the hostess prior to the party other than meeting her at a previous show when she made the booking. Thus, with the sales being so high, I felt a little more hesitant to refuse the setup she was orchestrating. There was a friend her husband worked with… yadda… yadda… yadda… she just knew he would be perfect. I agreed to meet this guy. She invited us over for dinner and a game. It seemed harmless and I did need to keep the client happy.

I went there not thinking too much about it. I do remember exactly what I wore, a pair of 501 jeans with holes in the knees, a pink cropped sweater and a pair of high-top tennis shoes. He wore a very bright, almost neon orange color tank top. And a pair of
shorts. He was not the type of guy I normally dated. He was taller than me, but he was quite thin, like stick leg thin. He did have good biceps.

I felt comfortable with him so we did have a good time talking. After the dinner we ended up playing a game from this book she had called The Book of Questions. I don't remember exactly what the rules of the game were but somehow this book would give scenarios where each player would have to say what they would do in that situation. It was basically a gauge of what the player's morals were. For example, if you were in a situation where two people were bit by a rattlesnake, you and another person, but only enough anti-venom for one, what would you do? How would you handle it? And why? I think the goal was to try to match your partner.

Corey and I were partnered together, and the hostess and her husband were partnered together. Corey and I were doing well; they were doing horribly.

As the questions went on, the funny thing was Corey and I realized we pretty much had the same morals. We weren't sure she had any. We were able to laugh about that and we became pretty fast friends. We started talking on the phone quite often.

I, at that time was not interested in anything other than friendship. And he seemed to be okay with that. The first time he asked me on a real date it was to a rodeo. He had bought tickets and they were probably not cheap. He got the dinner and the rodeo package. I had to cancel at the last minute. One of Chris' surgeries had some complications. I ended up having to stay in Los Angeles longer than expected.

The second time he asked me out for date, I don't remember why I couldn't make that one to be very honest. I don't know if it was because it was the time when Chris was sick and I was having to give him IV pushes every four hours, or if I was just blowing the date off. I hope it was the former, but it probably was the latter.

Somehow, he was not put off too much and we continued to talk on the phone a lot. Eventually we ended up going places and trying to make them not really dates. He loved archery, so he took me to the archery range, and I got to see how he shot his bow. I didn't know then but learned later on, he was a very skilled archer. He has lots of plaques and animal mounts on his walls proving that, although you would never hear him brag about it.

He was in the military. At that time, he taught heavy weapons. So, he played with the real big guns and had kind of a fun life.

To me, he was just my friend, and I would talk to him about the other guys I was dating, they weren't really good guys. I wasn't really serious about any of them, I was more just trying to see, you know, what would turn out?

The only time that it ever even crossed my mind to think about him other than a friend, was every once in a while, we would have a little argument because he'd say something that sounded a little bit like jealousy. I'd end the discussion with the comment "Hey, you agreed to be my friend, you know. I'm not breaking any promises. I told you that's what I wanted." He'd agreed to it.

Then one evening as I was getting ready to go out, Chris said to me, "You know Mom, I don't get why you don't marry Corey. He's the only one I like to be around when you go out on your dates (Oh my word! I'm so embarrassed. I forgot that I had him babysit while I dated other guys.) He's the only one I have fun with and he's the only guy that you are with that makes you happy." He was seven.

That kind of shocked me, because at that point I was like "Chris that is not, no way, no that's not what's gonna happen." But it did plant a little seed.

Not long after that, Corey and I planned to go to a drive-in to see the latest Terminator movie "Judgement Day." We had Chris in the back seat. Corey asked if I wanted something to eat. I, completely oblivious, didn't realize that it was a couple days before he would be paid again. He was using the last of his food money. (He was particularly good at staying within his budget. A quality I have really appreciated over the last 31 years.)

We went to the concession shop and got the most ridiculous things like bonbons and licorice, (I had never ordered those things at a movie before or since.) We also got popcorn and drinks and maybe we even each got hot dogs. We lugged all the food back to the car, fed Chris as fast as we could so that he would go to sleep so we could watch the movie.

I don't know if it was the bonbons or what, but during the movie, unlike any time before with him, I wanted to kiss him. I hadn't ever wanted that before. I hadn't even considered it. So, using my normal tricks I started to flirt a little bit. In fact, I got really
flirty. I started to play with his knee a little because he was wearing jeans with holes in them. I would touch him a little more often to make contact. Eventually I was pretty much just leaning over and throwing myself at him.

He wasn't going do it. He would not kiss me. That got me. The next day he came over after work and I could tell there was something on his mind, he was bothered. There was something on my mind too.

After some small chit chat and making sure Chris had something to entertain him, we went out on my back porch balcony. I sat on one of the walls and he was sitting where I could see him, but only in my peripheral vision. He started to tell me that basically he didn't understand what was going on last night. He felt the relationship was getting too hard because he wanted more than friendship and I made it very clear, other than my
behavior the night before, that I only wanted to be friends. I responded with, (and I'll admit I was very, very afraid to say it,) "But what if that person that only wanted to be friends changes her mind?" He sat up straighter and looked over at me. "What do you mean?" And I said, "Well last night I really wanted to kiss you."

I could not see his face full on, I could only see the peripheral. But there was no way to miss the smile he got on his face. I kept my face turned. I didn't let him know I'd noticed right away, but I saw it. He said "Well, maybe that should be discussed. Maybe it could work." I said, "Well I just did, and I think we should try it," fully expecting to turn around and have him kiss me.

That guy came over the next three nights in a row and would not kiss me one single time. He knew how to play too. Finally, the fourth night he came over, we put Chris to bed, and we started to watch a little TV, just sitting on the couch talking. It was getting late, and I knew he would be leaving soon. Another night without a kiss.

The Arsenio Hall Show came on at 11:00 p.m. signaling the time to go. We weren't talking about anything special. I think by that time we had moved from the couch to the floor because I only had a 12-inch screen TV and you had to be pretty close to be able to see it.

I don't remember who the guests were, but I do remember the next part. As Arsenio introduced the number, "For you here is 'Keith Washington, singing Kissing You." I turned and looked at Corey thinking he was going to say goodbye for the night. He kissed me. And the minute our lips met, the song from the TV started playing, "Kissing you". It was so perfectly orchestrated. It was the most amazing kiss there ever was between two people. I love the kiss described in the movie Princess Bride. It always makes me laugh because, such was our kiss.

And I knew without a doubt at that exact moment, that he was the man I was going to marry. He didn't know it at the time. I'm sure he didn't even have a clue. But I knew.

We kissed a lot that night. And then he left. It was so wonderful.

He kissed me on July 14th, and we got married on October 5th. Our wedding was held in the backyard of a friend's parents. It was a small affair.

I wrote this, the evening I had my vision.

Corey,
I love, love, love roller coasters. The scarier the better.
You get sick entering the parking lot of an amusement park.
Somehow, we got together.
God performs miracles so often that we take them for granted,
But I don't on this
We rode the toughest ride with the highest of highs and the lowest
of lows
At the end, we still respect, appreciate and best of all, love each
other.
That's a miracle!

Eternally yours. I love you.

"Without love I wouldn't believe
I couldn't believe in you,
and I wouldn't in me without love
I believe in Love"
-Believe-

Chapter Twenty-Nine
Pre-Wedding Jitters?

"Help me dear Father to freely forgive,
All who may seem unkind to me."
-Help Me, Dear Father-

I've always said, "Corey chased me until I caught him."
However, over the last 30 plus years, I think we've both
done some chasing and catching. The odds were really not in
our favor from the very beginning. Corey was 26 and had
been married twice before. I was 28 and had a son. Maybe it
was because we were in Vegas, but poor odds weren't going
to stop us from gambling. That is until…

Corey's parents and sister flew in two days before the
wedding. Trying to get in good with the in-laws, I moved
out of my Condo for a few days. Chris and I stayed with
friends. (That was not ideal, and I would never recommend
it.) Our wedding was very much a low budget wedding.
That doesn't mean it wasn't lovely, it absolutely was. It
meant that all the work would be done by me, my friends
(Big Time) and Corey.

I didn't even get to pick out a wedding dress. My mom went
to a Gunnysack Outlet store and bought me a dress for
$75.00. It was an embarrassingly 1980's look, but whatever, it
was only a couple years out of date. A friend had a white

brimmed hat that we taped some netting and ribbon to for a veil, and I found a lacy pair of gloves at some
lingerie store. I had never even put the whole outfit on to see if it fit until it was time to
dress for the wedding. I even had to have Kalene's mom take off her slip so I could borrow it. Yes, I 100% looked like I had stepped out of a Madonna music video.

I bought my shoes. I paid for our marriage license in quarters that I had won at my bachelorette party. A friend from church owned a flower shop. She gifted me my bouquet and got the silk flowers for the rest of the bouquets and boutonnieres at a
good discount.

Oh, and poor Carma. She made me my wedding cake and, on her way to put it in the car, it fell on the ground. Of course, Carma being Carma didn't even tell me, until it was all over, so I didn't have to worry. She ran to a store to try to get some kind of cake. There just happened to be a three-tier wedding cake that someone never came to pick up. It even had some flowers in my wedding colors, rose and turquoise. She bought the cake, put some of the flowers we had to decorate, on top, and it was perfect. (Although, I've seen the things Carma has decorated and I know the one she made was probably better.)

We decorated the back yard with white balloons and candles. Then we wrapped ribbons of rose and turquoise around wreaths with some of the silk flowers. I am absolutely sure my friends did far more than I am aware of.

The plan was to decorate, set up chairs and prepare for the rehearsal dinner the afternoon before. Then on that night we would do a quick rehearsal, eat dinner and get married the next afternoon.

The first time I met Corey's parents was when I was helping with the decorations. Corey was to come help set up the chairs. He was late. Finally, he arrived with his mom, dad and sister in tow. He brought them in to meet me. Of course, my friends all stopped what they were doing to watch the introduction. They assumed I would then introduce them to my about to be in-laws and we would all get back to decorating, appreciating the extra hands. That is not what happened.

To say his mom was "icy" would be very kind. So, I should probably stop there. However, this is a tell all book. Let me paint the picture. The only time I ever really dreamed of or even thought about marriage throughout my teenage years and into my
twenties was to have another family I could be a part of. In fact, I can even recall a time I was yelling at my mom telling her I couldn't wait until I could leave my family and be a part of my husband's. I had come close to getting married two times before. Those parents loved me, especially the mothers.

Not to mention, but I guess I'm doing just that, I had let them have my house during a time I really would have liked to have my own room with my own bathroom and my own make-up.

Her "Hello" was absolutely vicious. There was no hug, no "Welcome to the family," not even "It's nice to meet you." I, walking towards her with my arms raised thinking there would be some sort of embrace, immediately put my arms down. I looked over to his sister and she had the exact hatful expression on her face. (In fairness to her though, she was a teenager. She grew into a delightful woman.) I then looked towards Corey's dad. His eyes were a bit down cast, but he did put an arm around my shoulder and softly said, "It's nice to meet you."

Corey then took me aside and told me he was taking them shopping and was going to show them around. I was completely incredulous. When I began to say "O…kay… but are you going to set up the chairs first?" his mother immediately let me know that "Corey, would be taking them shopping." Then they left.

My friends, who had witnessed the whole thing, seemed to be in as much shock as I was. None of us even spoke for a while. We just very silently went back to work. At last, one of my friends uttered, "What the hell was that?" I looked up and they saw the tears streaming down my cheeks. Of

course, they all stopped working and spent the next half
hour consoling me and picking her apart. We decided to just
blow it off. Maybe she wasn't feeling good, or just wasn't
good at meeting people for the first time…etcetera…
It really unraveled me, though other than the tears, I didn't
let on how much. Something was off with Corey as well.

My family arrived later that afternoon. We held the rehearsal
that took up about ten minutes, then prepared to eat. It was
set up buffet style. I'm almost positive my mom brought the
dinner. If she did, then I have no doubt it was delicious. My
mom was a good cook. I didn't have any. I'd become a bit
queasy. This wasn't just the night before the wedding jitters.
Something was not right.

The only interaction I had with Corey's family at all came
just as a friend, probably Carma or Kalene, convinced me I
should eat something. As I stood waiting for whoever was
ahead of me to finish dishing up their plate, Corey's mom
came up to me. I could see my friends do a side glance to
watch. Pushing my instincts, the ones that told me to find
any reason to get out of there, aside, I steadied myself. I
actually entertained the thought that she was coming to
apologize that she didn't welcome me to the family. I
was happy I hadn't picked up my plate yet. I would need
both hands to hug her and assure her it was not a big deal.
That is not what happened.

She walked up to me, and in a very low deliberate voice (I recognized the tone she used, it was the one my dad used when he was very angry. It's probably close to the tone I've used on someone I've chosen to despise) my future mother-in-law, the woman I thought I would get to call mom and cook for the holidays with, said to me, "I will tell you exactly what my mother-in-law told me on my wedding day. As long as Corey can stand to be with you, we will stand to be around you when you visit." Then she turned and walked away. She never said another thing to me that whole visit.

Within seconds I was surrounded by friends and sisters, though not in any obvious way. They did not leave me alone the rest of the evening. I don't think I was even able to talk to Corey until he came back to get me after taking his family back to MY house in MY car because his was a sports car that they wouldn't all fit in.

Do I justify her behavior? I wish I could. Did she grow to love me? No never. She took emotional and mental abuse to a new level. I will say I love her because she did raise Corey to be a very good man. She was a good grandmother to my kids. However, I learned that no amount of service, like taking her to her doctor appointments, having them to Sunday dinner every Sunday after we bought them a house so they could be closer and we could help them; nor would gifts homemade or store bought, ever make her treat me kindly. (Although she did like that I worked at a jewelry store).

I can think to myself now, "Well… it was her loss." It definitely was. Still, I was the one who suffered the consequences of her actions. I've tried putting myself in her shoes, she had been through two daughter in-laws already blah, blah. I had been married to her son for over 25 years when she passed. Though I would turn myself inside out to try to please her, I never did. She never said a kind thing directly towards me. The best it ever got was "Ok well we love y'all" as she was about to hang up the phone when Corey had it on speaker. Of course, my daughter was in the room with us.

Corey has defended me on many occasions even if I didn't really need it. But not to her. I think by the time he realized just how bad it really was he thought it was too late to do anything. If that is the reason, he was probably right. She chose to hate me before we even meant. When they moved back to their old home, I no longer felt the need to go with Corey when he went to see her, so, she no longer needed to stand my visits.

And that's all I'm going to say about her.

"Rotten peaches, rotting in the sun
Seems I've seen that devil fruit since the world begun"
-Rotten Peaches-

Chapter Thirty
Let the Church Bells Ring

"Through the still small voice the Spirit speaks to me
To guide me, to save me, from the evils I may see…
Listen, Listen, the Holy Ghost will whisper
Listen, Listen to the still small voice"
-The Still Small Voice-

When Corey and I were finally alone after the rehearsal
dinner things did not improve.
I think the first words out of my mouth to him was
something like "What the (insert expletive) what did you say
to your mother about me?" He told me that they had an
argument the night they got there, but they had fun
shopping. I told him what his mom said to me. Corey said
nothing. Our drive to his car was pretty much just me
crying, then yelling and him saying nothing.

When it became clear he was not going to say anything to
his mother, all my hurt became anger. I'm like the
"Incredible Hulk" no one likes me when I'm angry, or more
accurately when I go into rage mode. I knew I carried the
same genes that my father had. I worked very hard to keep
my anger in check. When I realized he was not going to be
on my side I exploded. I ended up hitting him in the
stomach. Absolutely the wedding was off! We drove in
compete silence for the remaining minutes to his car.

Like I had said before, I had come close to marriage before. I knew how to call things off. My brain was just filling with reasons for why marrying this guy was a bad idea, none of my own thoughts were kind. But there was another voice, that was drowning my thoughts out. A feeling came over me; the same feeling I had when I was leaving the hospital after I had delivered Chris. I was about to make a life choice that was going to take me very far off course.

I was still very… very… angry. He started to get out of my car. Then I could neither hear, nor even think another thought except for "Get him back in your car."

Get Him Back In Your Car!!!

I recognized the voice. It was the Holy Spirit telling me to get him back in my car.
Usually, my spiritual promptings weren't given to me at full volume. But time was of the essence here, so I was getting full force. It was so loud that I didn't even argue with it (yes, sometimes I argue with what God asks me to do. He always wins the argument and I end up doing it, but I still sometimes make the attempt.)

I put all my pride aside and I pleaded for him to get back in the car. He wasn't going to. I think back on those few seconds. It seems like so many life altering events are those where there are only a few seconds to choose. I'm so very

grateful that I had been given many opportunities to learn to recognize when I was being prompted by The Holy Ghost to do something versus my own ever-cycling thoughts. I had also learned both
from following and unfortunately, probably even more from not following those promptings.

Any anger I had felt just a nano-second ago was gone. Gone was any feeling of pride, or any need to preserve my own "perceived" self-respect. The only thing I felt was a desperation to get him back in my car. Pleading and begging were two things I just never did, at least not with a man. I had, and still do, a lot of pleading and begging to God. But not a boyfriend for crying out loud.

But that night, in those few seconds, I pled, I begged, I entreated, beseeched, supplicated; anything just short of throwing myself to the ground and kissing his shoes (Hah I probably would have even tried that). Eternity played out in those few seconds. He got back in the car.

Then suddenly I didn't know what else to do. I kept thinking "OK Now what?" Nothing came. I definitely knew the source guiding me to get him back into my car.
Thus, the only thing I could think to do was pray. Corey agreed, he could at least do that. I could tell that though he had agreed to taking things to the Lord, his mind was pretty much decided. There would be no wedding in his near future.

We drove to a little place that overlooked the city giving us a spectacular view. The prayer was a very simple one. I don't even remember who said that prayer. We asked if we were supposed to get married. The experience we shared will remain between Corey and me. It is quite sacred to us. What I will say, and the reason for sharing this part of my story is that the confirmation was so strong and given to us in such a way that we could not then nor ever in the future deny it. We were to be married.

And so, we were. And when the tough times came crashing down, when others would have cut and run, we've always "got back in the car."

The wedding was beautiful. I walked down the aisle to the theme from Somewhere in Time, I sang Funny Valentine, (the Barbara Streisand version with the more flattering lyrics.) we even had comic relief from a June bug that was flying around scaring me to death, best of all…

We both said I do.

> *"Nobody told us, cause nobody showed us*
> *Now it's up to us babe, oh I think we can make it"*
> -Don't Go Breaking My Heart-

Chapter Thirty-One
My Kyle

"How sweet to hold a newborn baby
And feel the pride and joy he gives
Greater still, the calm assurance
The child can face uncertain days because He lives."
-Because He Lives-

Earlier, in the letter to my mother, I referenced how hard it was for me to feel good about my pregnancy with Kyle. I really wanted to be happy. The people around me were happy. Corey and Chris were thrilled. I couldn't figure out why I wasn't feeling the overwhelming joy that I thought I should be feeling. I still avoided seeing myself in the mirror. I tried very hard to believe that Corey did find me beautiful even when I
was hugely pregnant. But I couldn't see any "pregnancy glow,"

The pregnancy was quite a normal one. I did suffer from nausea, but that was manageable. There were absolutely no complications with his delivery, other than I had to be induced because he was two weeks late.

I loved him. I loved him while I carried him. We had an ultra-sound done so I knew it was a boy. I participated in all the fun things leading up to his birth. I just had this big part of me that couldn't chase away the phantom pains of guilt and shame. This caused me not to bond with him as quickly as I had with Chris. Perhaps, I thought I needed some miracle like an angel to make me feel this child was indeed mine.

Absolutely, I wish I knew then, what I know now. I hadn't even begun to address the grief I felt over my first three pregnancies. My despair was now less about the loss, I had begun to put that into a different perspective; though I still grieved it was a different kind. My anguish was because I had not dealt with the grief over the way I was treated just being pregnant. Pregnancy was a shameful obvious sign that something sinful had taken place. And though there was absolutely nothing sinful, quite the opposite, in being pregnant with Kyle, I still was suffering mentally and emotionally from the past experiences.

Kyle cried a lot more than Chris did as a baby. Part of that was because I was trying to nurse him. I wanted to do the best thing and was told that was it so that's what I did. However, and I do believe this is part because of the trauma from past pregnancies, unbeknownst to me, I wasn't producing very much milk, so the poor kid was always hungry. Once I switched to a bottle, he was a happy little baby boy.

There were other differences between the boys. Where Chris was very content to play with his toys alone, or just read a book, Kyle wanted to be with somebody all the time. He did not like reading and was constantly active. Still, when there was no one to play with he had a fantastic imagination to entertain him. For example, when he was about three, he started playing with his thumb, index finger and middle finger shaping them as birds. He would then have the two birds interact with each other. I can't count the number of times I would look down the church pew at Kyle and see "his birds" having an all-out war with each other causing a huge distraction.

He also could play for hours with the erasers used to put on pencils. They were great armies conquering the world.

Most wonderful, I'd never met another kid born with such a gift for compassion and forgiveness. All throughout his life he kept that attribute. No matter how many times he would be angry with someone or was really hurt by another, Kyle would forgive and forget instantly if he received an apology. When Kyle wouldn't get the apology deserved, he would think about the situation from their point of view and forgive and forget. I valued that trait and have tried to adopt it into my life; it's not an easy one to develop.

I'm so glad that each kid was different because it caused me to stretch and grow as a mother. Things I used to teach, entertain and even discipline Chris, had absolutely no effect on Kyle. So, I had to learn another way to parent. The boys were eight years apart, so it was almost as if I had two only children. This allowed me to develop skills easier than those who have kids born closer together. The disadvantage was that they seldom played together, the gap was too big.

I could tell stories for hours about my kids. Don't worry, I won't. There are a few things raising Kyle did that had a huge impact on me.

The first was that I, with help from my therapist, was able to realize that the shame of past pregnancies needed to be addressed and worked through. That took more work than one might think, or at least more than I thought. I discovered that a lot of it was also tied to the poor body image issues I had. Sometimes I still have to work on that part.

The second, was because Kyle was so active, I was constantly told to put him on different medicines. I learned that I could not just take the word of a doctor. It was up to me to study out the medicine suggested, weigh out the side effects and then make a responsible decision. Being a part of government medicine meant being treated by protocols, not by the individual.

The third was patience. Kyle was my opportunity to practice what I preached. I had to be even more dedicated to finding healthy outlets for my anger and frustration. I also realized I had to pay very close attention to the "why" of his behavior. If I was able to address the cause, we would be able to avoid so much of the bad choices to follow.

Because of Kyle I was also able to learn to appreciate Corey as a father. He did not take his anger out in violence. He never abused the kids. He showed them love. It was not shown the way I showed it, which was great because… well they were boys and needed male thinking… but also, they got all kinds of love

The wonderful thing, something I was unaware of at the time, was the more I appreciated the kind of dad Corey was, the more I was able to feel a little more appreciation for the kind of mom I was. Each time my muscle for patience grew for Kyle, it grew for myself. And learning to study medicines would be a necessary ability for the rest of my life. And my shame at pregnancy just went away the longer I got to be Kyle's mom.

Kyle is my philosopher. We have had the most interesting conversations. He is one of the few people I know that is not afraid to investigate new ideas and really delve into someone else's thinking. He discerns his own truth and then grows in his faith and knowledge. He's further ahead in his mental and emotional journey than I was even close to being at his age. I hope my experiences helped him.

I have promised my children that I would tell as little of their stories as possible, using only events that pertain to me. Because of that, this next section may feel like it's lacking some detail.

Kyle got married to a woman who had two children. One of the boys was almost 18 months when we met him, the other was just maybe six weeks or so. I absolutely adored those children. I loved them with all my heart. I found out that every great cliche made about being a grandparent was true. I think I was a pretty good grandma. I did all the things I heard grandmas did. It was such a pleasure to have them in my life.

About five years later, the marriage would end in a messy break-up. Because Kyle was not their biological father, and they never had the money, nor felt the need to have him legally adopt them, our family was no longer allowed to have those boys in our lives. We could have no contact. I don't think I can even write a word or sentence that will convey the grief I felt at losing them. I guess I'm still trying to process it. I think it's
still too raw though it's been a few years.

I think one of the biggest take-aways I've learned, both through my grief and through the vision I had, is that I will not be spared from the pain of other's actions. That does not mean I have to internalize it and morph it into a situation where I should have done something to spare myself or others. Just because it hurts, even when the pain is almost unbearable, that does not mean I am responsible or that I am guilty. It is just a consequence of mortality.

"Is the nightmare really black or are the windows painted
Will they come again next week; can my mind really take it?
-Madman Across the Water-

Chapter Thirty-Two
Corey Teaches Me

"Help me teach with inspiration.
Grant this blessing, Lord, I pray.
Help me lift a soul's ambition
To a higher, nobler way."
-Help Me Teach with Inspiration-

Just like the rest of my life matrimony would not be easy. As beautiful and as rich as our marriage has been, (And I can't even think of the words to say how good it is now, although I might try later in my story,) it has taken a lot of work. I think that if asked, anyone that has an incredible marriage, would totally agree.

One of Corey and my favorite sayings is,

"A successful marriage requires
falling in love many times
With the same person"
-M. McLaughlin-

In fact, we each have a mug with that saying on it. That is definitely how it's been for us. I knew from that first kiss. Corey, you know, he was a little slower I think, although maybe he knew the whole time and was playing me, because he certainly secured the hook before he reeled me in.

With both our baggage, it was a hard blend. Marriage, at least my marriage, is/was not for the faint of heart. It took a lot of patience and understanding; a lot of compromise; a lot of learning; a lot of growing.

Neither of us knew how to be married. I knew I didn't want what my mom and dad had for sure. It didn't occur to me until many years later that Corey probably didn't know any more than I did, after all he had been divorced twice before.

It was especially difficult for me to really trust Corey when he got mad. It was less about me being afraid he would hit me, I knew how to take a punch, so to speak, and had learned since the aforementioned Dallas incident, how to fight back. What unnerved me was the way he got angry. I'm a yeller. I came from a family of yellers. I've heard a lot of people yell, especially the married ones. Two out of three of my kids are yellers. I was used to people yelling when they were angry. That's what "normal" people do. (At least that's how I saw it.) When Corey was mad, he'd go silent. There's nothing worse for someone that yells to solve issues, than someone who refuses to say
anything. I learned to recognize the level of his anger by how tightly his teeth were clenched and how much his cheek twitched.

One day Corey came home from work. I don't have any idea what we were arguing about, or even how the chain of events started. I perfectly remember my reaction.

This is how the scene was about to play out in my mind. He was about to hit me. He was very angry. There was no way to get through the front door because he was blocking it. I knew I wouldn't have time to dash to my bedroom before he could get ahold of me. I braced myself for pain. He was about to hit me, there was no escaping that. I knew it was really going to hurt my back when his punch knocked me into the countertop. The only way to avoid that pain, which I knew would hurt worse than the punch itself was if I were on the countertop.

My excellent plan of action...I quickly took off my shoes and while throwing those at Corey, I jumped up and sat on the countertop, skillfully avoiding hitting my head on the cupboards above, closed my eyes and braced for impact. There was no pain. Wait, what? I opened my eyes to see Corey looking at me like I had suddenly grown a third eye. "What on earth are you doing?" he asked disbelievingly. He was flabbergasted that I would even have the thought that he would hit me. And then seeing the humor of the situation he added, "And did you really think that throwing your shoes at me would stop me?" We did both laugh and he still teases me every now and again about that.
"Are you going to throw your shoes at me?"

But of course, the one area that presented the biggest challenge was all forms of physical intimacy. I loved Corey. I loved him the best I knew how to love during that time. But I could not understand the concept of "making love." It just seemed like a silly way to put sex into a song. Corey wanted to kiss, hold hands, rub my back, and even just hug. I was very uncomfortable with that. For me, (and please forgive me for my bumbling here. I'm trying to put this as respectfully and cleanly as possible) I enjoyed the sex. I just could not connect the two. The only need for physical touch was to get

to the sex part. It did not have anything to do with love for me. That was very difficult for both of us. I'm sure it was extra confusing for him because I did like to kiss and hold hands when we were dating.

Actually, I was also confused. That's what boyfriends and girlfriends do. They kiss and hold hands. I didn't see married people holding hands and kissing. The closest thing I saw was when a man would lean forward, putting his elbows on his knees at church and the wife would rub his back. And quite frankly, that was a bit gross to me. And really what was the point of just making out when you're already married and can just go all the way? At least that's how I saw it then.

However, I felt, somewhere buried very deep inside my brain, that Corey was right. There should be love if there is sex. I shouldn't be flinching when he reached over to gently pat me or freak out when he tried to hold my hand when we watched TV. I really wanted him to be right. I needed for him to be right. I just didn't know if I could merge the two. I certainly wanted to raise my kids so that they could see their mom and dad loved each other.

I also couldn't understand why Corey wasn't just satisfied, even happy, that he was married to a woman that was up for sex any time he was. Why wasn't that enough. I thought that was what all men wanted. Why was he insisting everything should have love involved.

He could not understand how a woman who obviously liked to have sex never wanted her husband to gently touch her back in the kitchen or showed irritation when he tried to hold her hand while sitting on the couch. Or why I wouldn't return the whispered, "I love you."

This wasn't just a different love language or just our preferred way to show our love to each other. This was me having a total disconnect between love and intimacy. I think that is the best way to describe it. I just didn't know how to be completely intimate. But I really wanted to be able to be intimate. So, I did what I always did. I bought books on the subject. I searched the scriptures. I talked to friends and really any adult married woman willing to talk about it (which, at least then, was quite rare.)

I began to connect the dots, but I couldn't seem to master it. There would be certain ways he would touch me causing me to suddenly go into freeze, fight, or flight mode. Sometimes I would do all three. He might say something, or worse whisper something in my ear and boom I was out of there. Oh boy and if he accidentally tried the wrong new cologne; Forget about it. He was so patient.

I was so inconsistent; my reactions were so unpredictable; most of all I was so afraid I would never be able to love him the way we Both wanted. I've watched Corey work with skittish dogs and horses. He's skilled at putting them at ease, patiently earning their trust, then keeping them calm. Boy did I need a someone with that skill! I needed somebody to recognize that I was a kicked dog. I needed to be approached very slowly, very carefully, and so patiently. Corey did that. He did that for years; many… many… years.

He allowed me to learn. He held the space open when I just figured I was damaged goods and would never be able to get myself together. Each time I would cry because it seemed like I was taking one step forward, two steps back, he would assure me that no, it was the other way around, I was taking two steps forward and one step back.

I had very little patience and absolutely no patience for myself. He stayed patient enough for both of us. He would step back and let me grow, even when it was hard, even if I was angry that he was stepping back, because I just wanted to force myself better. He knew taking my time was crucial. He waited, watched me grow, then stepped back in, letting me be the new person who grew.

I recognize how rare just letting someone be the new, better version of themselves is. I've witnessed so often how hard it is for people to let go of the old person when someone is trying to change. Perhaps, I could have healed on my own, eventually. I know the Atonement of Jesus Christ covers us all. But I'm sure I wouldn't have been able to do it as completely without Corey. It definitely wouldn't have been as fun.

Eventually, I began to really learn and understand what love was, especially to comprehend how God meant for physical intimacy to be between two people that love each other. How He intended our bodies to join together in an ultimate act of unity, I could recognize what the experience would be like when both not only love each other, but completely trust each other, what it's like to be able to let go and not have any fear.
Not just to not feel fear but to feel safe.
Then to feel more than safe.
To feel secure. To feel loved. To feel adored. Corey taught me that.

And that feeling. that little prelude that Elton John had shown me. Ha, I didn't have a clue. I never imagined how wonderful my physical relationship with my husband was going to be. Yes, in the bedroom obviously, but more just how much I would enjoy his little pats on my back. Or that I would look forward to holding his hand when we sit next to each other.

I never believed it was even possible to feel safe, secure, protected and loved, even cherished in his arms in the afterglow. I didn't know "Making Love" was real.

Now. I am so grateful.

Only a loving Heavenly Parent would want me to feel this good.

> *"And I think it's gonna be a long, long time*
> *Till touchdown brings me round again to find*
> *I'm not the man they think I am at home*
> *Oh, no, no, no, I'm a rocket man."*
> -Rocket Man-

Chapter Thirty-Three
It's a Baby Girl

"I see my mother kneeling with our family each day
I hear the words she whispers as she bows her head to pray
Her plea to the Father quiets all my fears
And I am thankful, love is spoken here."
-Love is Spoken Here-

After the stories I previously shared, you can imagine my surprise when after Kyle we started to try again for our next child, and it didn't happen right away. And then a couple of years later, I was only able to carry for about five months. For the next couple of years, I had miscarriages. I couldn't carry to term. So, for me, it felt like another instance where God was mean. And it hurt.

After how easily I got pregnant before, and then the times I prayed to have a miscarriage. God was not letting me have another kid now? I felt the time was right, I had a good family, had a great husband, but it wasn't happening for me. Eventually, I reconciled myself to that fact that we weren't going to have any more children. I decided I would go back to school. I wanted to finish my degree and possibly work part time. I also had joined a scrapbook group.

(Stepping out of story, I have to give a shout out to those women. I actually scrapbooked with them for almost 20 years. It was wonderful. I love those women deeply. OK stepping back in.)

But just as I began on this new course - "Boom," I found out I was pregnant… I was 35 years old. I'm not sure if it was because I had convinced myself that I was finished having kids, my age or if there were some residual unresolved issues, but once again my brain was defaulting to the old emotional turmoil.

One night after a day of being very nauseated, I had a dream. The only thing I could remember when I woke up was Corey holding a baby girl, giving her a blessing and him saying these words, "I give unto you the name Alyssa Louise." That was all it took.

I woke up so excited. I called her Alyssa from then on, though the sonogram would be inconclusive. People kept warning me, I might be surprised. But I knew.

However, this created some more issues for me to grapple with. One of the ways I justified being led to place the other girls up for adoption and not Chris was that I would not be a good "girl" mother. I was about to have a daughter. Did I deserve a daughter? Could I raise a daughter?

As I write this, I'm getting a bit embarrassed that even though I learned from my dream that God was aware of me, and was aware of her, there was still that struggle within me. All… everyone, of my doubts and fears about having a daughter completely evaporated the day I could not feel her move anymore. I instantly became attached not just physically, but emotionally, mentally and spiritually. I was terrified I was going to lose her too.

I'll skip the details, but it was a very difficult delivery. She was rushed into the NICU before I was even allowed to hold her. I had been prepped for a C-section. For some reason, I wasn't consulted, the OBGYN doctor, whom I had never even met until I was in the delivery room, decided to use forceps. That was an unfortunate decision because it caused a great deal of unnecessary damage to me and the baby.

Corey was then forced to make the agonizing choice of whether to stay with me or go with Alyssa. I was in bad shape, but I wasn't really aware of that. I just wanted someone to be with my baby girl. I wanted to be with my baby girl. So, I made the decision for him, "Follow the baby."

After getting me stabilized, I was moved to a recovery room. I was told I could not see my baby until I was able to walk on my own accord and use the bathroom. Yeah, right! When the nurse returned and saw that I had been banging my legs on the side of my hospital bed repeatedly to try to get the feeling back, she decided she'd get me a wheelchair. I got to see Alyssa, but I couldn't hold her. At that time, I couldn't even touch her because they hadn't figured everything out yet. She was covered with monitors and tubes.

By this time, I had sent Corey home to get the boys so they would be sure to see her. So, it was just me staring at my baby girl, praying with every ounce of energy I could that I would not have to lose another baby girl. I pleaded, bargained, and made all the promises I could beseeching God to make my baby well.

Corey brought the boys, and they were able to come in and see her. Kyle was six and Chris was fourteen. It meant a lot to me that we all got to be together. I kept praying it wouldn't be the only time. God answered my prayer. Not immediately, but in a beautiful way. One of the things I kept repeating in my prayer was "Please don't make me go home without my baby." It worked out that my health required the same hospital time that Alyssa's health required. We went home together.

They sent us home with some extremely serious antibiotics for Alyssa. They were so strong that a nurse had to come and take her blood every 12 hours. The third time a nurse came (it was never the same one), she was having a very hard time getting the blood. She just kept trying. I finally said, "you have one more chance and if you don't get it, get out." That must have scared her because she somehow got it that time, though it was not a lot. After she left, I got a call that it wasn't enough blood, and she was going to have to come back and get some more.

What that nurse didn't know, was that I had been deep in prayer since she left. I knew Alyssa had to get off that medicine. I had that warning coming in loud and clear. I told the nurse no, she could not come. I immediately got an irate call from some pediatrician telling me that if I did not allow the blood draws than Alyssa could not be on that particular medicine. I said that was my intention. That doctor was mad. However, Corey was none too happy with me either. I stood my ground.

When we took Alyssa into the doctor the next day, we got a different pediatrician. She was fine with that decision and gave us a more mild and more proven antibiotic. Many years later, Corey and I were watching an episode of "Grey's Anatomy." In it, one of the doctors had a child that was on the exact prescription they had tried to make me give Alyssa years ago. The medicine caused deafness. Corey, turned to me, and softly said, "Thank you. You knew." I didn't know the side effects, when I said no more. I just knew Alyssa wasn't supposed to be taking that particular medicine.

What I did know without a doubt was to heed the promptings of the Holy Ghost. I knew how to recognize it. I knew ignoring it would be dangerous. I was so grateful I could do that.

Alyssa was exactly the girl that I prayed for. We got to paint our nails on the couch together. She loved to dress girly. I had play dates with other little girls and their moms.

I was involved in her PTA. I even was the president one year. I worked with her elementary school choir. It was exactly what I had prayed for sitting with her in the NICU. I even began to think that I had been wrong about God. Perhaps that's a
bit ambitious. What I thought was I had done enough good things so that finally, God was pleased with me

And then sixth grade…

Sixth grade is a hard time for every kid. I'd watched Chris and Kyle go through it. I attributed Alyssa's change in behavior to that at first. But, getting her to go to school became more difficult every day. There was more going on than just puberty. A very trusted friend of hers, had been bullying her.

Though I recognized bullying was another a form of abuse, I found I was unequipped to deal with that type. Part of the reason was when I grew up, bullying was not really acknowledged. It was just part of growing up. When I spoke with my husband about it, he thought the same way. It took us way too long to validate how bad it was. We hadn't a clue what the damage would be. We did try to address it with her. We just didn't have the knowledge or skill to immediately know how to help her overcome it.

(Again, I'm going to step out of the story for a minute. Recognizing my inability to recognize and respond to Alyssa's abuse, gave me a lot more compassion for my own mother. I really thought I was prepared and had taught Alyssa all the ways to avoid abuse. I had many conversations of what to do if ever abused. It never even occurred to me that bullying was something to look for. Other than the one incident I told about earlier in my story, I had never been a part of, or had a clue to the devastation bullying caused. In that way, I understood how my mom may not have instantly recognized my abuse.)

When I plug the scenario with Alyssa into the part of the story where I explained how in my vision, I was shown each generation tried to improve, I can see the obvious similarity. My generation had bullies; they were just as mean and probably caused just as many problems. It was just normalized. So, it just kept getting passed down. My children's generation brought awareness to bullying and rightly recognized it as a
form of abuse. Now I see a generation taking steps to stop it. It makes me hopeful. I can imagine a world where abuse is wiped out entirely. OK stepping back into my story.)

If it had been any other kind of abuse, I would have known exactly what to do. It broke my heart that Alyssa was having to deal with abuse beginning at the same age I did. She became completely withdrawn when put in any social setting. At home she was an angry, raging girl most of it directed at me. We did our best to help her. As soon as I figured out the real issue and the horrible extent of the abuse, I went to the school. When they did not stop the bully's behavior, I took her out of school and started her in an online homeschool program. Not too much later we were able to move to a completely new school district.

I'm not going into the details, but we were able to seek out inspiration from Heavenly Father to lead us to methods that would work best for her.

Alyssa has grown into a beautiful woman. She has a very successful career. We've been able to develop a good, open and honest relationship. I've learned so much through loving her. Things were not easy for what seemed like a very long time. But watching her grow and overcome her trials has helped me heal so much. In always loving her, even when it took extreme effort, I also couldn't help but love some of the sides of myself. I guess that is what she taught me the most.

This is another expert written just after my vision.

"My mind is racing with a million thoughts and organizing them to make a coherent writing may be difficult. Most of all my biggest

fear is that everyone won't know how much I love them. I'm filled with love, the weightless joy.

It's as if each pound I lose physically is replaced with love, joy and gratitude. It's amazing and weird. I know it even sounds, for lack of a better word, 'corny.' Still, It is real."

As I reread each of the journal entries following each time I had my vision experience, I realized the thing I found most important was that the people I loved absolutely were sure I loved them.

Even though a great part of the vision was exhausting and a bit grueling, the feeling of a love so pure penetrated me. It was so powerful, It made me want to share it. I began to tell my family members "I love you," more often. Then, I would not finish seeing a good friend without telling them I loved them at some, hopefully many points.

And I wasn't just saying it. I genuinely felt it, more than I knew I could. I was realizing the more I loved, the more love I had for the next person. Most of all, as I did this, I began to feel a bit of love for myself."

"It's the circle of life and it moves us all
Through despair and hope, through faith and love
'til we find our place on the path unwinding
In the circle, the circle of life."
-Circle of Life-

Chapter Thirty-Four
ECT Erase Me

"Jesus, take this heart of mine
Make it pure and wholly thine"
-Jesus Loves Me, This I Know-

I wonder if Sigmund Freud would say, the reason I got my electroconvulsive therapy was to erase who I was because I was so broken. Of course, if that was the case, I was not aware of it. The more concrete story is that in 2012, I found it difficult to hold onto
all my fractured parts. My instinct was to run, and I began to make those arrangements.

However, my family felt that I would be better off in a mental institution. They were afraid I was going to kill myself. Something I would never do. There was no way. As hard as life had become, I wouldn't do that to my family and most of all, I knew it would not be a good way to meet Christ again.

I went to the mental hospital. I was diagnosed with serotonin poisoning caused by the huge dose of anti-depressant that I had been prescribed. I had been on that particular medicine since I had my third child and went to the doctor because I felt depressed.

I was only there for three days and diagnosed with complex PTSD due to multiple traumas. During that short stay, I learned two very important things. The first was that there are people way crazier than me. The second, there was a procedure, Electro Convulsive Therapy that would take away my trauma. My first reaction was absolutely not…because of my memories of Jack Nicholson in the movie "One flew over the Cuckoo's nest"…(By the way, if you haven't seen that movie, it's quite moving).

The Psychiatrist assured me that ECT was nothing like the movie. Then, they showed me a video. The clip painted a very pristine picture. The man was on a table in a big room without clutter. They administered an IV with sleep medication and a paralytic to prevent convulsions. They shocked him and five minutes later he was awake without any noticeable aftereffects and walked out on his own. I also read many case studies showing positive results, most of them were veterans being treated for PTSD. I knew that it was an extreme approach…but I was desperate.

I had been told that because of the serotonin poisoning, I could no longer take an anti-depressant. I truly believed I needed them. If I couldn't take a pill, how was I going to be able to handle my life? So, I relented.

The reality, was nothing like the video. I went through the ordeal three days a week for three weeks and then two times a week for three weeks. During that time, not once did I get to talk to any doctor and was not being monitored at all. After arriving with a designated driver, I was taken back to a room the size of a small bedroom with five patients on cots. I was instructed to go to the bathroom and then lay on the bed. Mine was always in the corner.

The doctor and the anesthesiologists regarded us as an assembly line. I could hear them treat each patient before me. A blood pressure cuff was used on our calves to prevent the paralytic reaching our right foot so the doctor could measure the convulsions.

I will never forget the sounds as they went patient to patient. The doctors bumping each other and hitting the beds because there was so little room. The flopping of the legs on the bed. The horrible science fiction sound of the machine measuring brain waves.
Was it successful?...it took away memories. I was erased.

The unfortunate thing for me was, one month before I began treatments, we had moved from a home where I lived for 13 years to a brand-new house in another city. Every time I would leave the new house, I would come home and sit on the couch and look around with no understanding of why I was there.

I recognized family members but couldn't remember relationships I had with friends or events that had taken place. By the third week, I really had no idea why I was doing the treatments. When Corey expressed concerns about the memory loss, we were told that was common, but they would eventually return, so stay the course. Corey had to watch his wife completely disappear. He did stop the treatments. He had to endure the fear, the hopelessness, the distrust and the other physical tolls I was experiencing. It was rough.

(I'm not against ECT even after my experience. I've continued to follow several studies. I am against the way it was administered to me.)

Some memories did return like a rush. Out of the blue, some little thing would trigger my brain to unlock the memory and I would relive the experience feeling every emotion, sensation, smell, touch, taste and sound…all at once. Thus, instead of forgetting traumatic events, I was reliving them.

But it did allow me to process the events differently. I was able to view them with a different perspective, placing less blame on myself. But it cost me.

I became a zombie. I was like the Walking Dead (not the eating people kind.) I still have very few real memories of my old house. Fortunately, I was a huge scrapbooker and was able to piece some things back together. I also kept a journal. Unfortunately, I used my journal as a way to get rid of negative emotions and reading it sent me into a tailspin. It seemed like the life I had lived was horrible. It was very hard on my kids. It was overwhelming for my husband.

And that is how I existed until 2014 when I had the vision.

> *"It doesn't seem a year ago to this very day*
> *You said I'm sorry honey if I don't change the pace*
> *I can't face another day."*
> -Love Lies Bleeding-

Chapter Thirty-Five
Later That Night

"If that isn't love, the ocean is dry
There's no star in the sky and the sparrows can't fly
If that isn't love, then heaven's a myth
There's no feeling like this, if that isn't love"
-If That Isn't Love-

As I have been writing this book, I have also been studying the Old Testament. I have been very mindful of two things as I've pondered over what I've read. The first were the women I will share what I have learned from them in another place. The second were the visions given to the prophets, specifically the way they tried to explain their visions.

It is very hard to interpret things shown in a Heavenly Sphere to something understood here on earth. I've learned to really understand requires a great deal of preparation and then submission to the will of God. I was able to witness so many concepts, some just to get a better understanding of what I had already studied, but the bulk of it was very new to me.

I was given very specific instructions at the end of each of the four times I was shown the vision. In the first vision I was told to study specific concepts. I was also told to do some specific acts. Some of the commandments were very symbolic.

I performed each of the symbolic acts I was told to do. I didn't fully understand them at the time. Even after being given the revelation the second and third time I just went by faith. I did what I was told to do and walked in the dark, confident that the light would be turned on when I was ready and in God's time. I won't share all the emblematic deeds I was told to perform. Some are too sacred to be shared here, or maybe at all. I do want to share a couple of examples.

After the first vision experience, I was told to get a blessing to seal the things I'd been given during my vision upon my head. This would also be recorded in Heaven.

Receiving a blessing was not a new concept to me. One of the marvelous parts of my religion is that those having Priesthood Power (the authority to act in God's name) can give an individual a blessing for the things the person needs, and that God wants them to have.

The simplest example is giving a Priesthood Blessing to the sick. In that blessing The Lord may instantly heal the person, give comfort or even let the person know that they have fulfilled their mission and are ready to return home to the presence of God. I find it especially beautiful because it allows a man that is living righteously, in total submission to the will of God, to use his Priesthood Authority to bless another. To me that is as Christlike as it gets.

What I was struggling to understand was the need for that blessing. Or maybe a better way to put it is that I wasn't sure of the purpose. The answer came in the blessing I received. This is an excerpt from my journal, just after I had received the blessing.

"The priesthood blessing, I received through Chris and Corey was beautiful. Corey anointed my head and Christ did the sealing. Before they did, I said a prayer and tried to describe some of the things I saw in my vision. Chris shared a scripture that had come to him that day out of Job and a quote by Elder Holland regarding the wounds remaining in Christ's hands after resurrection.

It went perfect.

Then he gave me a blessing. In his blessing he did lock-down 'reconciled the events of last night and my place there and now' he also said to write and that my writing 'shall be a scripture for future generations of my family.' He warned me that my trials were not over. He spoke of the great love my Heavenly Father has for me.

Now, going forward, I was to search in the scriptures for the many examples of those who erred and then repented and became great leaders. He said they seem to be amongst God's favorites. He said that I 'stood amongst the noble and great ones shoulder to shoulder'."

The symbolic act was for me to request and receive the blessing. I had already been given some of the promises in my vision. But performing the act allowed me to not only have a greater comprehension of what had been revealed to me, but also teach it to others. I wish I could explain it better than this. I only know to refer to Ezekiel, the prophet of the Old Testament. He had to do a lot of symbolic acts. Some were quite difficult. But it was a concrete way to show the people that God was warning them.

Asking Corey and Chris to give me the Priesthood Blessing also showed my willingness to submit to the will of God and not to my own understanding. At the time my family had pretty much disintegrated. Corey and Chris hadn't spoken for months, Kyle was married, and they had gone their own way and Alyssa was also having serious struggles. To be perfectly honest, the last thing I wanted to do was share the sacred
experience with them.

It wasn't that I didn't want to share what had happened to me. I did! I wanted to shout it from the rooftops. I was just afraid that my family would trample on the experience. It did not seem possible to me at the time, that any of them would believe me, nor did I think we could all even be in the same room together without fighting, and that too, would destroy my sacred experience.

So, I stepped into the dark when I asked Chris to come over and join his dad in giving me a blessing. It was scary. The reward was beyond my wildest dreams. My family has never broken apart since. Though we would all go through some very difficult trials and often did the "two steps forward, one step back" dance, our relationships deepened. If I knew that would be the outcome I would have walked through Hell for
as long as it took. I'm so grateful that I just had to step into the dark for a few hours.

I was not only healing, but I was also beginning to thrive. Here is my favorite journal entry from that first experience.

"All is as it should be. Father and son were reconciled to seal blessings upon my head. My mind is slowing to a more tolerable pace. Still, lots of thoughts but softer.

Funny how such an incredible event occurred. And yet life continues in such a normal way. I still feel as if I'm floating a little above it all. Corey is down watching TV. Alyssa is laughing with her friend over the phone. I remain calm and know all will flow in time. Time - that finite thing that goes against an infinite plan with all eternity.

I am still so physically sick yet, I'm bursting with spiritual renewal. I love myself.

I sat on my tub edge and looked into the mirror. There I was. There she was - that girl in that exact position. Same tilt of the head, beaming. I couldn't help but smile big. 'Good for you'. I said to myself, as the past combined with the present in an instant saved picture for God's scrapbook."

> *"And you can tell everybody this is your song*
> *It may be quite simple but now that it's done*
> *I hope you don't mind; I hope you don't mind*
> *That I put down in words*
> *How wonderful life is, now you're in the world."*
> -Your Song-

Chapter Thirty-Six
Healing Doesn't Happen Overnight

"More purity give me, more strength to o'er come
More freedom from earth stains, more longing for home"
-More Holiness Give Me-

My quest to find my "loving Heavenly Father," became even more earnest after that first vision. An outsider might say I was a slow learner. But, to my credit, I did keep searching. All forms of healing take time. I had a lot of things to heal from.

Physically, I was quite sick. I knew that in order to reach my potential and become "whole" I needed to do what I could to heal all the areas of my life. The spiritual side was going forward at a steady pace. So, I began the journey to try to get better physically.

I don't feel the need to go into great detail about my health issues. I did have a great deal of wounds that needed tending. Some of my issues came from taking bad advice from doctors who really never took the time to see me. Some were from poor surgeons, some were from the way the ECT was administered to me, and some were because I had not dealt with the other sides of my life, so it metastasized into my physical body.

Corey and I felt very prompted during a visit to see Carma, to see what Las Vegas had to offer. Looking back, it seems like a "no-brainer" that I would begin to heal physically there. After all, that is where the rest of my healing began. We were inspired to get out of the American medical rat race and explore more traditional options. That worked well for me.

I had a great deal of success with Eastern medicine, such as acupuncture and herbal remedies given to me from a trusted doctor. But the best results came when I was able to merge both Eastern and American medicine. I was very fortunate. We were able to afford to pay out of pocket for these treatments, because our insurance covered none of it. It set us back a bit financially, but we've been blessed.

There was a healing in just allowing all that money to be spent on my health. Of course, I wouldn't bat an eye if it were Corey or one of my kids, but spending that kind of money on myself, caused me to stretch and examine my value in a very finite way.
There have been a lot of miracles along the way.

I worked very hard to be healthy. I'm still having to work very hard. Some of my major health problems have returned. I will continue to fight. But this time I feel no resentment about my health. I know I have done all I can do, and the rest is up to God, and I trust Him completely.

However, if asked a year ago would I be angry if I got this sick again I, if being honest would have answered "Yes! Absolutely. I've worked hard. But things changed after my third and fourth time being allowed to re-experience my vision. I view it now as only a consequence.

I was able to establish a medical team I trusted. I continue to benefit from those relationships.

When I had done what I could do with my physical self, it was time to concentrate on the mental part of myself. I had done a lot in that area already. Most of what I had to do was just become more diligent in the practices I had learned throughout the years. Mental health is such an interesting concept. I began to view my brain in the same way that I viewed my body. It would require the same amount of exercise and supplements. I implemented those requirements into my daily routine.

There was one thing that I did differently that has been one of the most beneficial healing practices. I learned how to meditate. I mean I did, still do the whole bit. *Ummu.*

It took a lot of practice. It requires a great deal of discipline. But once mastered, it can be a lifeline in any situation. I learned how to meditate for an hour. I learned how to do it in just 30 seconds.

After learning meditation, I was able to control most of my anxiety issues. I no longer must endure the long stretches of my racing mind feeling out of control. I've become adept at recognizing when I'm at the very beginning of the spiral. And in the same way that I've learned to listen to the promptings of the Holy Ghost, I've learned to pay attention when my mind prompts me to stop and give it a rest.

Meditation is the key to that. The moment of stillness during a good meditation session is so comforting. And now that I've developed the skill, I've been able to stretch it and combine both mind and body for healing.

Meditation has become one of the ways I feel most whole. It has become, for me, a period of time when my spiritual, mental, emotional and physical selves are working in perfect harmony to give me what I need in that moment.

I'd like to share an example from a more recent journal entry.

"So, I just did a meditation called "The Seed" from the podcast <u>On Sovereign Wings</u>. It was different than the normal ones that I do, in that it had you inhale light instead of just focusing on the breath, which was really nice.

And then it took you to your favorite place, a special place and mine is the beach at Galveston, that I picture so perfectly.

The exercise was to picture myself as a Goddess walking up to the "me" I am now. Our minds were to be open to what ever thought came from that first meeting. When we met, the Goddess fell to her knees and said, "I am so grateful for you and for what I/ you did. Because what you are doing is required to be what I am."

It was interesting because last night I was telling Corey how much I needed to feel appreciated. I didn't and I didn't know how to do that with myself because the only one who can appreciate me right now is me.

The things I'm doing are not really things other people will see like cleaning and organizing. It was so refreshing to have this happen this morning, the very next day. I just didn't know how to appreciate myself."

It's pretty profound, to see how my mind immediately recognized my perfected self would be grateful for the work I am doing now to improve myself.

With the spiritual, physical and mental healing underway it was time to focus on the most difficult one for me, emotional. The emotional healing required me to really have to face my feelings about my Heavenly Father.

"And I don't know what the time is, or what the next line is

Or how you're gonna take the news
But if I had my life again, I wouldn't change a thing
I'd let nobody, I'd let nobody, stand inside my shoes."
                                        -Someone's Final Song-

Chapter Thirty-Seven
Sing! Sing a Song of Praise

"When peace like a river attendeth my way
When sorrows like sea billows roll
Whatever my lot, Thou hast taught me to say
It is well, it is well with my soul."
-It Is Well With My Soul-

In 2018, I can recall very distinctly sitting at my desk doing my college class work. I was getting certified to teach English as a Second Language. The assignment I was working on required me to list things that once were assets but now considered to be a liability. We then were to examine each thing listed making sure we were realistic in determining the difference.

I began to list some of the obvious things, like a rental house we once lived in, now had been a drain because the tenants kept destroying things; automobiles that had been in an accident; tangible assets. We were then to write a short paragraph describing how we felt about the liability. This took some creative writing because I really didn't feel particularly bad or good about any of those things.

But the one asset that I really mourned was my voice. It was for me, the tangible asset that most affected my life. I had used it to make money. I used it to do my callings at church.

I used it for my pleasure. I used it to get through difficult emotions such as anger, betrayal, heartache and any other facet of my life. It was the core of who I was, kind of everything to me.

Though I chose to have a family and forgo a professional career, I still had many opportunities to use my voice in church and community events. Most of my music focused more towards things that had to do with faith. So anytime I could sing at church. anytime I could get a position in church which allowed me to lead the children in singing or teach the youth how to direct music, or even direct the music in our congregational meetings, I jumped at the chance.

But my most favorite position became leading the adult choir. At first this surprised me. I always was the one performing. However, I found so much satisfaction in, not only sharing my love for music, but also in seeing them begin to love it the same way.

I did have one choir that was so special to me. It had a lot of adults that loved to sing. However not all of them could sing well. As most choir directors discover, those are the voices that seem to sing the loudest. I really worked that choir. I had little tricks that I had learned throughout the years to help them harmonize. By Easter we performed a beautiful Cantata and it sounded awesome. It meant so much to me because as I directed them, I could see the joy on each choir members face. They knew it was so much more than they ever imagined.

I realized how much better it was to be the conductor. To show people their potential and bring that potential out of them inspired me much more than my own performances. I never would have dreamed that would be as fulfilling, let alone more fulfilling than performing myself. I was able to do that for many years. It was a great way to not only get to know others, but to let others get to know me, (at least this side of me which was my favorite.)

However, as I began to get sick it got harder and harder to stand on that stage. First of all, I couldn't control my body temperature, so I was usually shaking to death by the time I sat down. Then, after holding my arms up to lead for periods of time, I would be
thrown off balance and so I would have to have my husband or one of my children accompany me off the stand. It wasn't that big of a deal at first, just a little embarrassing. It was in front of the entire congregation.

My illness progressed. I could no longer stand up for very long periods (like 3-4 minutes at a time.) I conquered this by getting a bar stool to sit on. Then I could no longer keep my arms above my head, so I would direct less enthusiastically.

But the devastation came when I could no longer sing at all.

Singing was who I was. At least it was the best part of me. It was how I regulated myself. It was how I showed love to my family. It was how I praised God's name. I didn't really know what to do without being able to sing. I couldn't even sing along with the radio.

This was kind of the straw that broke the camel's back. It seemed to me like every time I would begin to feel like there was even hope of finding the loving Heavenly Father I had been searching for, God would do something I viewed as mean. Taking away my voice was just cruel. Especially because I had used my voice to glorify Him.

A couple days later as I was finishing up my assignment and actually working on the paragraph where I was pouring out my sadness regarding the loss of my vocal asset, I began to weep. Writing the rest of the paragraph was out of the question because I couldn't see through my tears. All I could think to do was kneel and pray.

I believe the only intelligible words were "Dear Heavenly Father, what is the deal? How could you take away my voice?" Right then the phone rang interrupting my prayer. At first, I thought to ignore it. But I wasn't feeling much comfort form my appeal, so I
answered it. It was a church leader for a large part of the surrounding region.

He proceeded to tell me that the Prophet for the Church of Jesus Christ of Latter-Day Saints was going to be coming to our area. They were asked to put a choir together for the event. It was to be in the AT&T Center. Practices would be held in a church building about a 40–45 minute drive every Sunday evening for six weeks.

My brain was screaming with anguish. I can't sing, I can't even stay standing! Driving that far on a Sunday evening would be impossible for me. I was barely making it through the hour and a half of church on Sunday mornings. Oh, how unfair of you God when I was just crying to you about this exact thing!

However, the words that came out of my mouth were, "Oh my word! I am so honored. Thank you! I would love to! I will be there this Sunday."

The songs that we had to sing were not easy, especially for the first soprano part. Some of the notes were quite high and only a few could hit them. But astonishingly, I was one of them. And I was able to make every practice. By the time I got home from practice I was completely depleted. I would have to rest in bed all day on the following Monday. Oh, but it was so worth it.

The day of the event was a bit hectic trying to get the whole family there, which normally would have worn me out. I had to park pretty far away (I had given the good parking pass to my family so they could get good seats.) But I was able to walk all the way to the building, then all the way down to take my place on the stage. I hit every note, even the highest with a full voice. I was able to stand without even a wobble. I was even able to walk back to my car in the rain.

Yes, my prayer couldn't have had a more obvious and miraculous answer. I'd be lying if I didn't admit I wanted more. I hoped that if I performed as valiantly as possible the Lord would let me sing again, but that seems to be something that I won't get back.

So, if there had to be a last time I could sing, doing it with a choir of 50 people chosen from such a large area in front of 33,000 people isn't a bad way to go out.   I even got a fantastic picture of just me singing on the animatron. It's my favorite picture.

As I reflect now, I realize I have had many "once in a lifetime" opportunities to sing. Way more than my fair share. I'm a little embarrassed to admit I wasn't satisfied with what I already had got to do. I had actually sung for two other Prophets in choir's made up the same way. I don't know how I was so fortunate enough to make it into three. Very few people get to do that. It was truly a blessing.

I still forget the loss and attempt to sing a song that pops into my head because of something someone has said. All that come out now are squelches. That's a hard one for me.

Still, it has forced me to learn other ways to regulate myself, show love to my family and praise God's name. And now that I can't sing along on the radio, I have conversations with the people I'm driving with. I have no doubt that someday I will be singing in one of the choirs in heaven. Maybe I will even get to direct one. Until then, I will try to hold on to the experiences I've been fortunate enough to have and appreciate what I'm learning to do instead.

> *"And when that moment comes at last*
> *And you remember who you are*
> *Here I'll be – Shooting Star"*
> -Shooting Star-

Chapter Thirty-Eight
The Missing Piece

"Lift up your heart, lift up your voice
Rejoice again I say rejoice"
-Rejoice, the Lord is King!-

I have been trying to come up with a way to explain what it was like when I finally found the piece I had been missing when trying to heal emotionally. I think I described it best in my journal,

Journal Entry 3/2020

"Just listened to a podcast "Virtual Couch" w/ Tony Overbay. His guest was Nikki Eisenhauer. I feel like I'm finally validated. I'm not crazy. What a relief of momentous proportions. Thank God in the most reverent way possible.

So, I'm on my own self-imposed mental health retreat. But I couldn't relax. I've had quite a few blessings already. But I have to to mention this particular journey.

I woke up anxious. I really wanted to be able to just shut my mind down and rest, but it was impossible. I did every chore I could think to do here.......I set everything up and started trying to read "Let God Love You" by Wendy Ulrich. Couldn't get into it." (It is

a good book, and I did finish it. It was just not what I was to study at that particular time.)

"Finally settled on listening to a podcast that delved into some thinking I was doing. Knew I was hearing good stuff but not exact. Felt very prompted to look through prior episodes and knew when I saw it, this was the one.

IT WAS!

For the first time I heard someone describe my brain exactly how I feel and think in a superhero positive way.

And I knew it was true. I've known it all along, but I couldn't seem to communicate or ever be validated with it. I've sobbed and sobbed but in a real release way with just the joy of finally knowing I'm not crazy, I'm right.

I am a highly sensitive person and probably in the top 20% of those people."

(It is estimated that between 15-20% of the world's population is Highly Sensitive)

"So many pieces can come together. My mind is racing and I'm wanting to pace.

I have to take her class and learn how to control it.

I have to acknowledge I know God led me to this moment. I am so grateful; I need it so much!"

(If you want to listen to the actual podcast for clarification, it is "The Virtual Couch" Published February 4, 2019, Episode 104)

There are so many factors that came together allowing me to finally learn how to pull my emotional self together. I had been conscientiously trying to work on it for a couple of years by March of 2020. I just kept hitting a brick wall.

When my brother offered me the opportunity to stay in his house up North while he worked in California for a couple weeks, I jumped at the chance. Two weeks alone to do some uninterrupted research, you bet! Then I would get to see my brother when he came back up for a few days. I knew I'd go home with a fresh outlook and could ramp up my healing.

Like so many things in my life, events did not go as I originally planned. However, by this time I had grown a great deal in the other aspects of my life; spiritually, physically, and mentally. This made it so much easier to not just roll with the change in plans, but to kind of look forward to the way life played out.

I had brought a couple books with me dealing with emotions and a couple dealing with how our brains function. I was planning on doing the research to complete the original book

I was writing. I had intended on being able to wrap up the labor-intensive work and begin to organize all my notes into some semblance of a well-researched book.

God had other plans for me.

Journal Entry 3/2020

"I'm thinking of my life like I'm on the shore of a beach. If I look out into the water, I may see a boat I'd like to get on.

However, there is no dinghy or deck to just gradually get to the boat. The only way there is to swim out.

This requires constant energy to fight against the current. Anytime I stop fighting the natural rhythm of the waves, I get drug back to shore.

There is no opportunity to stand still. The tide will knock me over, cover my feet in the sand or just lull me into floating, but looking up and seeing I've been pushed way off course by some undertow.

One constantly has to keep swimming and moving, checking on direction.

The only chance of a rest would be if I could find a small island or dive below and rest on the bottom."

I knew I wasn't going to be able to wrap up my studies as soon as I heard that podcast. I was prompted to put that stuff away and do a deep dive into what it meant to be a "Highly Sensitive Person." The first thing was to get passed the name itself. Being "sensitive" was always presented to me with very negative connotations. I had equated it with being easily offended, something I had been accused of in the past and
something I had worked very hard at trying not to be.

Now, I was about to admit I was not only "sensitive" but "highly sensitive (HSP)." And I only had about 10 more days to comprehend it so that I could begin implementing the tools such knowledge gave me. I got on Amazon that day and ordered some books on the subject. There was no time to waste. When my books arrived, I got to serious work. Time was really running short. I only had just a little over a week to understand the topic, at least enough for me to know what to do with the knowledge. I put my phone on do not disturb mode, checking it twice a day to make sure everyone was fine and let them know I was. I did not turn on the TV and the music I listened to a playlist I had created over the past several years that put me in the "studying zone."

I was on a retreat. My family knew to only contact me if it was an emergency. I talked to my husband once a day, but it had to be brief. The rest of my responsibilities could wait. My usual retreats were only a week or less. I tried to get one in about every six months or so. Because this one was going to be closer to three weeks, I felt I really needed to bring back a substantial amount of healing energy. I was completely unaware of what was going on in the world.

This is my journal entry the day before the world changed.

Journal Entry 3/2020

"So much to learn, so little time. Brother arriving in couple days. See notes for study details."

I found the research fascinating. There were so many threads to follow. I resonated with the concepts as soon as I read them; I was able to see exactly how I fit. What I couldn't quite grasp was, other than validation, how was what I was learning going to help me with my emotional healing. If I only had more time maybe I could figure it out.

Now I'm not in any way implying that the happenings that would follow within the upcoming weeks were orchestrated for my benefit. What I will say is because I was at the right place, during the right time, doing the right thing, God did allow me to take advantage of the upcoming events.

On the 19th, I spoke to my brother. The governor of California had declared a stay-at-home order…And the rest… is history. I had an additional two weeks to process

my newfound knowledge…then I had another two weeks…
then another. I couldn't get a flight.

Corey and I were trying to make arrangements to have him
drive across the country to pick me up. Luckily, the airlines
started doing limited flights and I was able to fly home in
style. (The COVID restrictions for the airline allowed me to
have the whole row to myself. That was great.)

The extra time was put to good use. I was able to spend time
with Wayne and discuss what I was learning with him. It
was so helpful to get a male's perspective on all of it. Plus,
because he knew me since high school, I was able to really
talk through some other things I was working on.

I almost hate to admit it and I mean absolutely no disrespect
to the millions who had to suffer during 2020. However, for
me, 2020 was such a good year. My husband was able to
work from home allowing us some time to reconnect. We
drove through 37 states, which meant I only had four states
left to complete my 50-state bucket list.

I was also able to take a "Boundaries Course" with Nikki
Eisenhower, the woman from the original podcast. That was
so beneficial because I was learning how to set boundaries as
an HSP. I had never really explored that particular aspect
other than in context as a parent. Learning how to set
boundaries allowed me to safely merge my different

characters into one. It didn't happen overnight and took a lot of practice.

There was a lot of push back. But I did it. What a relief!

But most of all, I was seeing a light at the end of the tunnel that I had been in for so many years. There were still a couple things I would need to grasp. Still, I now was able to really know that healing was indeed a very real possibility. And I was in the home stretch.

> *"I used to be the main express. All steam and whistles heading*
> *west.*
> *Picking up my pain door to door.*
> *Riding on the story line, story burning all the time.*
> *But this train don't stop there anymore."*
> -This Train Don't Stop There Anymore-

Chapter Thirty-Nine
Still Standing and Still Teaching

"My heart can sing when I pause to remember
A heartache here is but a steppingstone."
-Until Then-

I am still learning from Elton John forty years later. One of the biggest lessons, I learned just recently reading his autobiography. At first, I was hesitant to read it, because … well … even Elton John said in his book, describing his meeting Elvis Presley, you should be careful about meeting your own heroes.

Over the years, I'd hear things or read something in the newspaper painting Elton John in unflattering ways. However, my rule is not to believe things unless it comes from that person's mouth. And if they are celebrities then I am doubly careful.

So, I've never really took too much to heart other than knowing that he had other points of view on a lot of things in life, but that's good, that makes it a really fun world.

When he released his autobiography, I finally said, yes, those are his words. Now… it was time I got to know him better. One thing surprised me, and it was enough to make me put the book down for a while. Elton John shared some of his experiences during the height of his cocaine phase. He used to get people together and get them high on coke and alcohol, then have them do things they would never do if they were sober.

I couldn't help relating to the people he was manipulating that way. And the devastation they must have dealt with the next day. I don't know how long some of them had to deal with that… embarrassment …shame. Did it hurt them like it hurt me…to wake up the next morning knowing you had been exploited?

Was my guardian angel someone else's abuser?

I had to put the book down for a while. I'd had to really sit with it. And I asked myself some really important questions.

When can an abuser be a good person?

Can a good person be an abuser?

And I really had to examine my own views… because throughout my whole life, Elton John had been my staple… the one that had always been there for me. The song that always came on. Still now… My natural Xanax

It took me probably a good month of deliberating over that… before I could even pick the book up and read the rest. I learned a lot from that. It was not something he was proud of. I appreciated the fact that he was courageous enough to reveal this ugly part of his life. He didn't go into any extreme details or insincere apologies… just a confession. This allowed me to learn about how to write my own underbelly of experiences.

I saw this as an example of someone who moved on from mistakes and ultimately improved himself. And I saw that is where he was…that's not who he is now. And that's never who he's been to me.

I could hold both truths in my heart. He was my guardian angel. And during part of that time, he may have been somebody else's nightmare. But he's not anymore. And I know. Because I do let filter in all the good things he does. I know how many artists he has helped, and the many people he's reached out to help them through addiction.

I know all that he did for AIDS. He fought to raise money and brought to bear political awareness and public education. He showed the world it was not just a plague God had enacted on a certain group of people - that a mean God had enacted.

So, after reading his book. I got to close it and again be grateful for the additional lesson.

> *"I'm still standing better than I ever did*
> *Looking like a true survivor*

> *Feeling like a little kid."*
> -I'm Still Standing-

Chapter Forty
Amazing Grace

"Twas grace that taught my heart to fear
And grace my fears relieved
How precious did that grace appear
The hour I first believed"
-Amazing Grace How Sweet the Sound-

Over the past several years I've had the tremendous privilege of serving as President of our County's Child Welfare Board. It definitely was a blessing to be able to give back to those who are fostering and adopting. It has also been so fun playing with the kids at fairs, group foster homes and other such gatherings. It has been a rare position or calling where no matter how much I gave, the blessings I've received were doubled.

Working with those that volunteer their time in the community on top of their work, church and family obligations, is absolutely amazing. It's where the best of the best dwell.

However, by far the greatest gift was the close association I've had with my fellow board members. I have learned so much from them. I love each of them dearly. There is no way to thank them enough. Almost exactly one year ago, they

gave me the very last lesson I needed to prepare myself for
all the things writing this story, my story, would
require.

I have had some wonderfully enlightening conversations
with those I've served with, especially with the other
officers. At one of those meetings one of them (and I know
she will not want me to call her out because she is so
humble, but she knows who she is) brought up the subject of
grace.

Of course, I had heard the word. I sang the song hundreds of
times. But I could tell the way she said it and implemented
it, that it was a much deeper concept than what I
understood. Over the next couple months, we would talk
about it. Yet, it wasn't until I experienced it from them that I
was able to comprehend what it really meant.

While 2020 was an awesome year for me, 2021 was not. Not
at all. I felt like I had been given all the correct tools, even
the correct supplies but could still not assemble a birdhouse.
Areas of my life that I felt were fixed, and ready to move
forward on, were suddenly falling apart. By September of
that year, I was feeling completely hopeless.

I knew I needed to take another mental health retreat. So, I
went to the beach, my place for renewal. In the past, by day
two of experiencing the sand and the ocean, I'm if not

optimistic at least neutral. However, this time I could feel nothing but discouragement.

Since 2020 our board was meeting over Zoom. I had brought all the stuff I needed to prepare the agenda and fully intended on conducting the meeting. I just couldn't do it. I'd hit rock bottom. I texted the other officers and said I couldn't do the meeting without any warning or time to prepare. I quickly received a text back saying no problem. The meetings were taped so when it ended, they emailed me a copy. I
couldn't open it for days. I was too afraid because I had let them down. When I finally got courageous enough, I opened up the recording and mentally prepared myself to hear their disappointment in me.

That is not what happened. Instead, I heard their love for me. They showed no trace of irritation, I was not blamed for the lack of preparation, nothing but thoughts of prayers and love. At that moment I completely understood the concept of grace. And probably because I was so discouraged, I was gently being prompted by the Spirit, not of times I had received it, instead I was being reminded of how many times I had extended it. It was as if God was saying, this is something you don't have to work on. You've got this. Recognize it.

The hopelessness was gone. What a gift they gave me by just being the graceful women that they are. I love you all so much.

"With a friend at hand you will see the light
If your friends are there
Then everything's alright"
-Friends-

Chapter Forty-One
I Didn't Know

"Then sings my soul, my Savior God to Thee
How great Thou art, how great Thou art."
-How Great Thou Art-

I mentioned that I started writing this book in 2014. Since that time. I've made a great deal of changes in my life. I learned so many wonderful things. Still, I was struggling with how to complete the commandment I had been given after my first vision. I couldn't figure out exactly how this book was supposed to come together, the format, the actual outline. I didn't even know how to begin, let alone, the middle and the end. Each attempt I made just wasn't feeling right.

So, once again God showed me.

On May 7, 2022, I was invited to participate in my sister in-law's baptism in New Mexico. I was so thrilled for her and felt honored that she would ask me to speak about the topic of the Holy Ghost, my favorite talk to give.

By this time, I had cut off all contact with my dad. Not really because I held on to any anger, it happened because in a specific moment I had a profound realization while attending my grandma K's funeral. I thought I had prepared myself for her death. We had said all we needed to say to each other, she gave me some great parting advice. She was 96 and over the last few years she had dementia and the last time I was able to go see her, she hardly knew me and I realized the grandma I knew was no longer there. So, I thought I had grieved her loss at that time. Yet, when the news came that she had died, I felt as if the world had opened up and swallowed me whole.

I will forever be grateful for the way my husband and children supported me through that time. We were able to drive as joint family unit to Phoenix where her services were held. A lot of really treasured moments happened on that drive.

The day after the service we were at my sister's house visiting. I tried to visit with my dad. He began giving me one of his tired lectures. I asked him point-blank, "Hey I've learned something new about that, would you like to hear about it?" He looked at me dead in the eye and said, "No not really." At that moment, I realized I had honored him in every way that I had been commanded to do. I really had no reason to have any contact with this man anymore. It was always painful to see him; It did nothing good for me; It was obvious that he had no need for me to be in his life and there is no reason why I needed to keep allowing him to hurt me.

It was so freeing. It was not out of anger, it was not out of an event, it was just out of a moment of realization. Wow! you don't need me. I don't need you, let's go our own ways. So, I stopped all contact with him.

However, at this baptism, my mom and dad were also there. I was prepared for that. My brother Ron kindly made it very clear that I wouldn't have to worry, I wouldn't have to be alone with either of my parents. My daughter was able to come, and of course, my husband gave me the same assurances. I knew they couldn't understand how at peace I was regarding my parents. The realization I had those few years ago,
really did allow me to step away emotionally.

Oh, but I so appreciated knowing that I had those people looking out for me. And true to their word, even down to the seating arrangements, someone was always there to gracefully swoop in each time it appeared that I would be alone with them.

The hard part for me was that by then I was beginning to have several "mini-strokes." I had gone through the same thing years before and had learned that through occupational therapy, I could train other parts of my brain to regain most of my motor skills and other areas affected. However, the strokes were beginning to be more frequent and stronger.

After the baptism we all went to dinner. We had a really nice time. Ron and Jesse invited a couple of friends so that it

wouldn't be just family to try to avoid any awkwardness. But, as we were about to leave, probably aided by my fatigue and some
extra emotion, I attempted to get up and couldn't, I had another "minor" stroke. I started shaking violently and then I lost all perception of where I was in regard to my surroundings. I didn't even know where my arms and legs were.

As my husband and brother carried me out of the restaurant, it became very obvious to my parents just how sick I was and the kind of things I was enduring with my health. Normally, with the help of Corey, I can hide most of my symptoms. This time it was in full display. My biggest concern at that moment was that I was afraid that Corey would not pick up my arm off the table across the room.

By the time they got me to the car, those I was with (we were the last to leave the restaurant) were focused on me. I couldn't figure out how to get in the car. I couldn't even imagine how I could possibly fit and what that even meant to get inside the car. Corey and I were trying to joke and make light of the situation. He knew that I didn't want everyone to witness what I was going through.

When they finally got me in the car and assured me that they did pick up my arm that had somehow got on another table and my other hand off the curb, there was nothing anybody could do but stick their heads in the car and give me a hug goodbye. It was an awkward hug because I couldn't return it, my arm and hand were in the back seat. So, I just sat there and allowed them to hug me.

I'm sure they were all scared for me and probably a little in shock. Like I said earlier, Corey and I had been through this a couple times before, we knew the science behind what I was experiencing (I won't explain it all here, but our brains are so fascinating.) So, we were less concerned. We knew that the best thing for me to was to get me back to the hotel so I could lay down and do the meditation necessary to retrain my brain to recognize where the parts of my body were and then determine where I was in reference to my surroundings.

Thus, it was unavoidable when my dad stuck his head in the car to hug me. I was perfectly comfortable with that. It was such a weird experience, because although I was dealing with my own serious symptoms, I was also keenly aware of the emotions of those around me. I could feel them stiffen up. But as my Dad came into hug me the only thing he could repeat over and over was "I didn't know. I didn't know. I didn't know.

And suddenly as he left the car I realized; he didn't know. There was no way he knew what he was losing when he gave over to that temptation so many years ago. There was no way he knew the relationship he was going to lose with his daughter, who had gone on to do all the things that would have made him proud. There was no way he could know the grandchildren he was giving up; the relationship with them, the relationship with a really wonderful man in my husband.

He didn't know. He didn't know.

He didn't know the damage that would be inflicted on me. He didn't know that he needed to take advantage of the opportunities that he had, been given so many times to seek my forgiveness. He had lost so much. He didn't know.

And then in that exact moment, I realized I didn't know. I didn't know I had confused what a loving father was, with what my earthly father was. I didn't know that I was basing my perception of who my Heavenly Father was on my earthly father who didn't know. In that split second, I knew I had to completely remove my earthly father from the equation. In all the confusion of that split second, my sense of who I was "A child of
God" a very loving Heavenly Father was born.

I went back to the hotel that night, and during my meditation I reexperienced my vision for the second time. At the end I was told that all my research was just for my own understanding. It was time to put it away and tell my story. The outline of the book came to me in a rush.

I am sorry that my dad missed out on so much because he didn't know. But I believe that it's our job to learn, to know, to grow and to become.

I couldn't wait to get started on this book. It has been difficult because I've had to recover from those strokes and the additional ones since. However, I have felt such peace because I know that my extremely loving Heavenly Father would make it possible for me to complete my task.

When I got home and began recording this book, I was privileged to experience the vision a third time. That gave me even greater understanding of what the first vision meant. At the end of that third revelation, I was given specific instructions of who I was to invite to be involved in this project.

I had begun my healing journey after Beverly, a very dear friend shared her story with me. I'm praying that someone will feel inspired to start their own journey after hearing my story.

There was one part of my vision that I kept getting wrong. So, Heavenly Father had me experience the vision a fourth time. It was that picture, the one He kept showing me to calm me, the one that I had tried to duplicate after my first vision while sitting on the edge of my bathtub. I thought He said, "This is my favorite picture of you." I kept thinking "of

course it is. I was perfect then." It wasn't until the fourth
time that I
understood. What God was saying, what He took the time to
repeat to me over and
over in the fourth experience was,

"This is how I see you."

> *"How wonderful life is while you are in the world."*
> -Your Song-

The End

Epilogue / Empaths

I wanted to add this part to my story. However, after talking
with some of the people who have helped me bring this
book to fruition, I thought it would be better in it's own
place. Mostly because few people will resonate with it.
However, the few who do really need to have this be
articulated.

I mentioned when I described myself as a little girl that "I
could 'read the room' with complete accuracy." I was really
understating things. The more accurate way to put it would
be I experienced the emotions of others. When I was within
close proximity like the same room, I could tell exactly how
they were feeling emotionally.

The best example I can come up with is Deanna Troi on Star
Trek: The Next Generation. And therein lies the problem.
Those of us who have this gift are often "Gas-lit," because
those that don't have the gift laugh it off as some sci-fi thing.
I think part of that is them projecting their own fear.

Being an Empath is a real thing. There are people out there
everywhere and the degree of ability varies. If you have
been blessed with the gift, recognize it, develop it and use it
to help those around you! At the very least, validate those
willing to speak out. I believe that with each new generation
the number of empaths will increase.

However, there are tools required to make the gift beneficial and not harmful. This is a gift where boundaries are essential. They were crucial for me because the more I was able to unite my different characters, the stronger the gift became.

Here are three examples of how I experience being an Empath. The first is before I had learned about boundaries.

When I would go into a grocery store, as I walked down the aisles passing other shoppers, I would know what their exact emotion was and often the cause of that emotion. For all my life up until I fully embraced that I indeed was Empathic, I had been told I was being silly. Those things only happened in some alien sci-fi species. Thus, instead of realizing I was feeling another's emotional experience, I internalized it all, thinking I was just on an emotional roller-coaster and not the fun kind. I could never go into a Walmart without taking a Xanax first. It was hard enough to deal with all the constant beeping, the lighting and most of the time the chaotic way the shelves were.

I remember a specific instance in June of 2020. I went to my favorite grocery store. I was in a really good mood. My husband and I were planning our road trip. I just needed to get a couple of things to tide us over until we left. When I got out of my car to walk in, I donned my mask with a little bit of sadness. I wouldn't be able to smile at people. I couldn't even stay in the store long enough to complete my purchase. I ran out of the store leaving my cart in the middle of the aisle. The amount of fear that I was feeling was overwhelming. I got home, locked all my doors and went to bed terrified.

Since then, I've been able to learn about boundaries, and especially because I learned them from another empath, I'm happy to say my experiences are quite different. I can go to the store, feel other emotions and distinguish between what is mine and what is theirs. I no longer even check to see if I have an emergency Xanax just in case.

The second example happened today. I met up with fellow board members at the bank to switch the accounts for the new leadership. I left myself "open" to be able to feel how the ladies that I had grown to love so much really were feeling about the change. There was one new member that hadn't arrived yet. I had never met her before.

Many people were coming in and out of the doors. The minute the woman we were waiting for opened the door, I could feel her emotion before I even saw her. (Yes, I have learned how to filter specific people in while keeping others out.) She was very anxious. I have found that one of the best ways I can help someone with anxiety, especially if I don't know them is to just gather up my calm (light blue) energy and share it while taking deep steady breaths. It doesn't take long for them to match my breathing, allowing them to relax.

On this occasion though, I was with fellow empaths. I could see one of them becoming very anxious as well. When she said something, I immediately validated her and let her know that I was feeling it too and we were able to let the new member talk it out and feel the calming energy being sent her way.

The third and last example happened a few months ago. I was quite sick and so my sister came to visit. Though I have learned and practiced so much with boundaries, especially those dealing with my empathic abilities, I often lose control when I am sick, extremely tired or it is a family member. On this occasion all three impediments were there. During her whole visit I honestly felt like I was going insane. I was taking all the extra Xanax I had tucked away, it was crazy.

It wasn't until after she left that I was able to realize I wasn't feeling that way, all those around me were feeling that way. I wish I could have recognized it then. I'm actually frustrated that I didn't. The visit would have been such a different experience.

I hope these examples help another fellow empath to at least feel validated. My advice to anyone that is an empath, no matter what the degree, is to pray for the gift of discernment. Actually, everyone should pray for that gift nowadays. But especially if you have the gift of being empathic. The first step is to be able to discern your emotions from another's. Then practice…practice…practice.

Throughout my story I talk about my quest to be more Christlike or developing Godlike attributes…

I'll let you make the connection.

Acknowledgements

There is no way for me to list and thank all the people who have helped me with this story. I would have to go through every person in my entire life. Thank you to everyone that made me who I am.

However, there are some specific people that directly helped me put this book together who need to be recognized, in no specific order, Kalene, Carma, Ron, Jess, Lori, Gene, Wayne, Connie and Karen. Thank you all so very much.

I really want to thank my family, Corey, Chris, Kyle and Alyssa. Thank you for your patience with me while I was consumed with this book. Thank you for loving me in spite of it all. Thank you for your willingness to accept all of me and encouraging me to share my story with others. I love you beyond words.

Most of all, I have to thank my very kind, loving Heavenly Father.